L
I Tho
(if

LAUGH *!*
I Thought I'd Die
(if I Didn't)

· ❧ ·

*Daily Meditations on Healing
through Humor*

ANNE WILSON SCHAEF

Ballantine Books · *New York*

Library of Congress Catalog Card Number: 89-90929

ISBN: 0-345-36097-4

Cover design by James R. Harris
Text design by Beth Tondreau Design/Jane Treuhaft

Manufactured in the United States of America

First Edition: November 1990

10 9 8 7 6 5 4 3 2 1

Dedication

This book is dedicated to laughter and those who laugh and those who don't.

It is dedicated to those in recovery, those who aren't, those who refuse to be, those who know they need to be and aren't, and those who don't know they need to be.

Have I left anyone out?

Introduction

I come from a family where the quip, the tease, and the practical joke are all part of the daily fare. We spent a lot of time laughing and playing as I was growing up. The humor in our family was always done lovingly with a lot of tenderness that could be easily felt. We never knew when a practical joke was going to be played upon us and there was *never* an edge of hostility or anger which I have since learned is present in so many families. We were a simple family that didn't have much money but we sure had a lot of fun.

There was an earthy "hillbilly" flavor in our family and our humor. This sense of humor has carried through my life and is, I believe, one of the greatest gifts I have had from my parents. One of the greatest encouragements for growth in our family was being lovingly teased into a new awareness. Hence, I grew up learning to laugh at myself first and then to laugh with others at our human foibles without any judgment being attached.

In my family, we took life seriously and we also played with it. Often what could have been turned into a tragedy or holocaust was turned into a giggle or a guffaw. A flat tire that became a picnic; my mother's single-handed dismantling and packing of our campground because she thought she heard a mountain lion in the bushes; the time we were stuck in the sand up to our axle; or the time my mother, father, boyfriend, and I took a jeep trail in Oregon in our sedan too early in the season and my dad got out to see why we were stuck (it was dark!) and stepped into an icy puddle up to his crotch and uttered the first and last swearword I have ever heard from him— "Damn!" We had to spend the night in the car, but not until we faced the suppressed giggles that kept the car shaking and had a good laugh about my father's one foray into swearing. All of these incidents became family lore, told over and over (often embellished over the years) as we laughed at ourselves and each other.

Consequently my work is laced with a lot of

laughter. I think that somewhere down deep I intuitively believe that humorless people are really dangerous and, at best, I just don't comprehend them. So, at my speeches, in the intensives, at the trainings, and in my life there is much humor, much laughter, much "cutting up," and great one-liners.

Hence, you can imagine my delighted relief when I discovered that people in recovery were *funny*. They laughed at themselves, they laughed at "*the* disease," they laughed at *their* disease, and they shared jokes that only recovering folks could understand. At first, I thought that some of the humor I heard in recovering circles was a little tough or hard. After a while I realized that it was tough and hard because it was true. Good humor is usually profound. And profundities are often best accepted when they are uttered humorously!

I saw how healing the recovering humor was. For example, Sam Meier (Serenity Sam), a well-known speaker and humorist in recovery circles, tells the story of an amazing Alcoholics Anonymous group he experienced early in recovery. "That was an amazing group," he states. "We had one guy in the group who had a kid who was sniffing gasoline. He would come home and find him passed out on the lawn and he would say, "That damned kid, I don't know whether he's dead or vapor-locked!" Gallows humor? One had to be there to get the full impact. Humor is really only possible if we personally know that place. Or Sam talks about a time when he had been in recovery for several years, was attending meetings and working the Twelve-Step program of Alcoholics Anonymous, and in spite of that (can you imagine?!) was slipping into a suicidal depression. One night after a meeting he decided to go home and kill himself (usually not a topic for humor!). He drove the car into the garage, left the motor running, and went into the house to write three (count them) suicide notes. He shares that they became a little more extensive than he had expected (surprise!), and then he did the dishes, as he didn't want to leave a mess. He then went out to the car and lay down in the backseat—but he realized he had to go to the bathroom and he didn't want anyone to find him with wet pants (no control issues here!), so he went in to go to the bathroom. When inside, the phone started ringing and he couldn't resist picking it up. It was a "newcomer" to Alcoholics Anonymous in a depression. Well, he could not resist telling him about the joys of sobriety and . . . now he tells the story.

Rather strange fare for humor, one might think but—not if you've been there. As the humorist and essayist C. W. Metcalf says, "Humor is about perspective—a willingness to access joy even in adversity." These are my kind of folks! I felt at home and loved the laughter. Sue Tysoe Myers says in the *Journal of Journeys,* "Acknowledging our experience of knowing our perfection is a giggle. The giggle is beyond the realm of the physical, mental and spirit, it's the pure joy of being."

As I experienced the fun in my work and the hilarity (sometimes!) of recovery, I thought we needed some daily meditations that were funny, captured the humor and joy of recovery, and made recovering humor available to all of us.

I like many of the meditation books that are out, *and* they are so *serious.* This book is not meant to replace them, it is intended to *complement* them. As C. W. Metcalf says, "You need to take yourself lightly and your problem seriously. You are not your problem."

So I thought I would try my hand at some daily meditations that were laser-light (and, perhaps, laserlike). At first I wanted to call the book *Each Day a New Giggle* or *One Guffaw at a Time,* but my agent and publisher thought I might get into trouble (what a new experience!) for being irreverent (hardly seems likely). So this book, *Laugh! I Thought I'd Die (if I Didn't),* came into being.

There is a meditation for each day and the meditations also are coded according to topic—whichever meets your needs or (if you don't have a need, where did you come from?) whatever meets your fancy.

There are several sources for these pages. I have picked up comments at meetings or at the intensives I do. Sometimes they are credited as "anonymous" or with a first name or first name and initial. I have gleaned some jokes, stories, and comments from "old-timers" at meetings, on tapes, and at conventions. Credit is given where possible. I have also taken the wit of some well-known folks and focused it upon recovery, and I have used quips that have come to me over the years and as I was writing this book. Special mention needs to be made here of Mark Twain, Will Rogers, and Bob Burns, who came from the part of the country where my roots are. I grew up with their humor, and they were mentors for me. When I started to work on this book, I uttered a little prayer—"I'd like a little help, please"—and the jokes started coming so fast that I was giggling until 4:00 a.m. that night until I begged for some rest. I have had many companions on this journey, both seen and unseen.

So here we have it. A meditation book based upon humor for recovery. As C. W. Metcalf says, "Someday we're going to look back on this and laugh." Why wait?!

· 🌿 ·

January

A Happy New Year

My isolation is the darkroom where I develop my negatives.
—ANONYMOUS

Drinking alone is isolating. Celebrating New Year's Eve with other addicts is also isolating.

The New Year can be a time for connecting with ourselves and others. Our negativism kills intimacy.

It could be fun to be positive about my lack of negativism this year. Happy New Year!

Humor

A chuckle a day may not keep the doctor away, but it sure does make those times in life's waiting room a little more bearable.

—AWS

Sometimes we are only able to see the seriousness of our disease and our recovery. We work hard and forget that humor is fun and part of walking this human pathway. Humor and healing go hand in hand. We cannot do one without the other. As we recover, we have the opportunity to experience the laughter and joy around us and within us.

· 🌱 ·

May I open myself this day to the chuckle within, the giggle without, and the laughter and joy that are everywhere.

Suffering Skills

Just because I do suffering well doesn't mean that I have to do it.
—MARYLU

It's important to have skills and talents in this life. It's also important to remember that we don't have to use them.

· ✥ ·

When our best-honed skill is suffering, we'd better get in line for some new skill training.

"Trusting"

*Want to get a good laugh out of an Alanon:
Just say, "Trust me."*
— JOHN PAUL COOKLEY

"Trust me"—our favorite words! How long it has taken us to learn not to trust people who can't be trusted.

· ✣ ·

To trust or not to trust—that is the dualism, and dualisms keep us stuck.

Shaping Ourselves Up

I was too busy worrying about my past and future mistakes (which could make me ineligible for enlightenment) to work on loving myself in the here and now.
—MICHELE L., AS QUOTED IN *Recovering*

If I could just get myself shaped up. I've got the prescription, I've been told what I *should* look like, why can't I do it? Doesn't work, does it?

• ❧ •

Prescriptions are different from solutions. With prescriptions, someone else or something else does it to us. With solutions, we have to immerse ourselves in them and do it ourselves.

Awareness

I still have to go to meetings. Sometimes I need a Seeing Eye newcomer to get me there.
—SAM MEIER (SERENITY SAM)

Twelve-Step work increases our depth perception. If we start getting too big for our britches, some newcomer will always bring us back to reality.

• ❧ •

I can't possibly see into a place I haven't been, but there are a lot of places I have been that I haven't seen.

Blame

What kind of insurance does a codependent buy? My-fault insurance.

—Anonymous

When we do not feel good about ourselves, we want either to take no blame at all or to take all the blame. We are people of extremes. Unfortunately either position is very self-centered. No matter what happens, we believe that we have to be the center of it.

• • •

The problem with sobriety is that it probably means *no* insurance.

Miracle of Recovery

Some days I just don't feel like working my program—then it works me.

—AWS

Sometimes we become so focused on the knowledge that our addictions are cunning, baffling, powerful, and patient that we forget that sobriety is equally cunning, baffling, powerful, and patient. If it weren't, recovery would never happen—and something seems to be going on.

· 🌿 ·

Today let me be aware of the miracle of recovery and that it is working in me—sometimes even in spite of myself.

Helpers

I had high blood pressure, so I went to see an M.D. He said that I was an overeater and wrote me a prescription for the most wonderful little pills you ever saw. So I went home fixed to take the pills, lose weight, and stay drunk.
—DAVID ORONOFSKY

It's amazing how many people—especially professionals—are standing by ready to help us. Unfortunately those who want to help us are usually helping us to kill ourselves.

• ❧ •

Beware of "helpers" offering fixes. They's often tricky sons-a-bitches.

Listening to Ourselves

When I get upset about someone not listening to me, I'm usually not listening to me.
—PEGGY

Listening to myself requires a lot of me. I have to stop, I have to believe I'm worth listening to, I have to give up all that internal noise so that my self can get through, and I have to notice what is going on within me and what I am saying to myself. Well, that's a lot, but not nearly as much as constant clitter, clatter.

· 🌿 ·

What a novel idea! Listening to myself.

Relationship with H.P.

I was having a romance addiction with my Higher Power. I wanted it to speak in tongues, get flashes from above, and in general present others with an impressive show of power.
—ANONYMOUS

When we want a flashy, impressive Higher Power, that's a sure way to get a gentle, steady, quiet Higher Power. A sense of humor isn't limited to the human species.

• 🌿 •

When I quit trying to define what my relationship with my Higher Power should be, I start having one.

Recovery Process: Options

Some days early in my recovery it seemed that it just wasn't worth it to get out of bed. Of course, staying there didn't seem to help very much either.

—AWS

Recovery is not always linear, nor is it always easy. However, when we think about it, neither has our disease been a barrel of laughs.

We have to remember that recovery is a process—one step at a time, one day at a time. If we only take the next step and keep coming back, it works.

· ☙ ·

Perhaps I do need to stay in bed after all. Maybe I'm not ready for options yet. One has to be careful not to move too fast.

Caution

I try not to get too close to someone until I get to know them.
—BILL

Not getting near someone until we get to know them sure makes relationships difficult, almost impossible at times. Not getting close when we *do* know them is even worse.

· 🌿 ·

When I get cautious, I get catatonic (the *C*-words). When I risk and reach out, I have relationships (the *R*-words). I'm early in recovery, but that doesn't mean I have to be early in my alphabet.

Prejudices

I hang on to my prejudices, they are the testicles of my mind.
—ERIC HOFFER

Prejudices get out of control just like raging hormones. A little bit goes a long way and even a little is too much.

· ❧ ·

Sometimes it's hard to find someone to look down on, especially if I'm getting near the bottom.

Recovering, Not Recovered

I have alcoholism, not alcoholwasm.
—DEAN C., AS QUOTED IN *Recovering*

How nice it would be to be recovered and not be recovering! But since life is a process and recovering is about life, I guess we'll just have to tolerate the recovery *process.*

· 🌿 ·

I keep trying to make myself a "finished product."

Truth

I've heard it said that if you're not working a Twelve-Step program, you're in denial.

—MARI

In an addictive society everyone could probably benefit from a Twelve-Step program. It's like the ones who need healthy food and exercise the most are the ones who avoid them. Take me for example.

· ☙ ·

Truth often comes in strange packages, and our packages get stranger when we don't face the truth.

Switching Addictions

When I first became aware of the Twelve-Step meetings, I could see that they worked, but I did not understand why. I decided to attend some "for research purposes" and then was faced with a choice of dying either from my addiction or from smoke inhalation.

—AWS

Addiction is addiction. We may switch addictions or practice a "lesser," "not so harmful" one. Aren't we funny? In the end any addictions will get us.

• ❧ •

I just don't want *other people's* addictions to get me. If I am going to be done in by an addiction, I want it to be my own.

Waiting, Being

Getting out of touch with my Higher Power is kind of like having a bad case of poison ivy. I feel like I need to scratch and often am much better off just waiting and letting it be.

—AWS

We addicts know a lot more about "doing" than we know about "being." Sometimes we think it is better to scratch a sore than to let it heal without our help. Can our Higher Power really be there if we don't control it? Is it possible if we take time to *do* nothing, we can *be* something? Do we use our busyness to keep away from ourselves?

· 🌿 ·

Today, just today, let me resist that haunting urge to *scratch.*

Living Skills

They have classes for learning how to play tennis and courses on how to write books, but where do I sign up to learn how to live life?

—ANONYMOUS

Often one of the side effects of our addictions or growing up in an addictive family is that we don't learn the everyday skills of life—how to handle money, how to keep the house in repair, how to keep *ourselves* in repair!

· ✸ ·

If recovery were as easy as signing up for a class, I'd have a Ph.D.

Chaos

I am a study of a man in chaos in search of frenzy.

—OSCAR LEVANT

Before we started our recovery, chaos and frenzy were ever-present possibilities. Now they are old friends who only drop by occasionally.

• ❧ •

Chaos is not a way of life (as some of us suspected). It is a way of death.

Impression Management

Be careless in your dress if you must, but keep a tidy soul.
—MARK TWAIN

Most addicts are more concerned with the external—it's called impression management. We think that if we just can control the way others perceive us, they won't detect our internal turmoil, and discover our best-kept "secret" addictions.

· ❧ ·

In recovery we learn that the external can only reflect the internal. In order to get a tidy soul, we may need a celestial Roto-Rooter. Prayer is the hot line for soul cleaners.

Being Where We Are

If I were wiser, I wouldn't be where I am now, but of course if I weren't where I am now, how could I get any wiser?   —AWS

S ometimes we forget that the best way to get somewhere else is to go through. We always want to get somewhere before we have done the process of "through." I can't possibly know where I've been unless I've let myself be there— wherever "there" is.

· 🌿 ·

It is in the going through that the wisdom emerges.

One Day at a Time

I have a new philosophy; I'm only going to dread one day at a time.

—CHARLES M. SCHULTZ

Well, one day at a time is a good start. Now let's look at "dreading" and try the one-*step*-at-a-time routine, starting with Step One. I could develop a "new philosophy" about being powerless over my dreading.

· ❧ ·

No matter how many "new philosophies" we try, they can always be used to reinforce our old "disease philosophy" until we begin recovery one day at a time. There's nothing better than a philosophical addict.

"We" Program

If one person tells you that you are a duck, don't worry, but if ten people tell you you're a duck, you better start looking for feathers around your ass.
— ANONYMOUS

One of the reasons that the Twelve Step program is a "we" program is that we need each other in order to see ourselves. As we hear others' stories, we begin to see through the veils of addiction. Also, we have come to recognize that others can see what we can't about ourselves.

· ❧ ·

I never thought of myself as a duck, although I *have* done a lot of ducking in my time—especially ducking the truth about myself.

Doing It "Hard"

It's not that recovery is that *difficult. It's just that sometimes I think it would be easier to be sitting on hot coals in one of Dante's circles of hell. At least, it would be cozy.*
—AWS

We always hear about how "hard" recovery is. We seem to forget how hard the disease is. How romantic to long for the dramatic, and our disease *was* dramatic at times. High drama and "hard" are intimately connected.

Once we start to reap the rewards of recovery, we decide that we don't need to return to "hard."

• ✣ •

Boy, am I good at "hard." Who would I be without my expertise?

Growing Up

Adulthood is a depressing destination. As you grow up, you become adulterated.
—C. W. METCALF

There's nothing wrong with becoming an adult. It's the *kind* of adult we become that's the problem. Besides, most of us don't have to worry about this anyway.

· ❧ ·

It's hard to grow up when we haven't grown in. I guess that's what growing up is—growing into ourselves.

Gratitude

Before I began my recovery, I thought being called a drunk (sex addict, codependent, workaholic, etc.) was an insult.

—ANONYMOUS

I used to think I had nothing in common with "those addicts." Now I'd rather associate with addicts than those who think they're not.

It's not hard to find other addicts. Finding *recovering* addicts is somewhat more difficult.

I know now that my recovery rests on calling a spade a spade (or a drunk a drunk), even when we are talking about ourselves.

• 🌿 •

Some people think recovering folks have some strange ideas. Being *glad* to be a recovering addict ranks right up there.

Grandiosity

Now when I see a red flag go up in a situation, I know that it means caution. Before I started my recovery, I thought it meant charge!

—AWS

My grandiosity takes many creative and varied forms when I am in my disease. The slogan for my grandiosity is "I can handle this!" I would plunge into situations and relationships where even a fool would know to go the other way. I hope this has changed. I *think* it has.

• ❧ •

Now when I see a red flag, I think it is an invitation to stop, think, and wave good-bye.

Focus on Yourself

Two things are bad for the heart—running uphill and running down people.
—Bernard Gimbel

I don't really run down people, but how about just a little teeny, insignificant, harmless observation sometime? . . . No!

· 🌿 ·

When I want to take someone else's inventory, that's usually a sign that I need to do my own.

Stinkin' Thinkin'

When I first started attending meetings, I asked what all those signs meant. I said what about Think, Think, Think? *My sponsor said, "In your case, it's with* What, What, What, *so forget it."*
—SAM MEIER (SERENITY SAM)

There's nothing like straight talk for crooked thinking. Of course it's *hard* to talk straight if you're thinking crooked.

· ❧ ·

When we are involved in stinkin' thinkin', it's difficult to notice that it's crazy and it stinks.

Illusion, Denial

*You know what's so funny about addicts? We
think we're not!*
—AWS

We addicts not only read "The Emperor's
New Clothes" as children, we made a decision somewhere along the line that that was a
preferred way of life. Gets chilly, doesn't it?

· 🌿 ·

Illusion and denial create illusion and
denial.

February

·❧·

Humor

I realize that humor isn't for everyone. It's only for people who want to have fun, enjoy life, and feel alive.

—AWS

When we are in our disease, we rule ourselves out of so many possibilities and our options get fewer and fewer. Ease, playfulness, and laughter have virtually vanished from our life.

Then, as we begin to recover, we start to see a giggle here, a chuckle there, and even laughter isn't completely out of the question.

• ❧ •

Suddenly my face muscles seem to be turning up instead of down.

Keep It Simple, Stupid

I believe in the power that created the universe. I pray every morning. My prayers consist of one word: HELP. That's it—over and out. And then I get up and do something.
—SAM MEIER (SERENITY SAM)

I t's the trying to pray "right" that gets us. As Sam says, "I spent a lot of years with a lot of prayers, and all of them were plea-bargaining and deals."

· ❧ ·

When we KISS (keep it simple, stupid) ourselves, our prayers follow suit.

Control-Con—Step Three

*It's not that I have that much difficulty
turning my life and will over to a Higher
Power. I just want to be consulted more often
about the speed and direction of the changes.*

—AWS

O nly in moments of extreme clarity are we
able to see that we are the only ones believing
our "letting go" con. At those moments we
can appreciate how really funny we are.

· ❧ ·

Grant me the awareness to see my *latest
level of expertise* with my con and the serenity
to laugh with myself about it. At least
let me *look* like I have given up my illusion
of control for the time being . . . Ooops.

Mistakes

Some of us, before we started our recovery, participated in a reign of error.

—ANONYMOUS

How difficult it was to admit we were wrong when we were wrong so often! Thank goodness recovery helps.

• ❧ •

The more mistakes we make, the more defensive we become about them. The more defenses we have, the more mistakes we make. Do you think there's a lesson here?

Not Getting Involved

How many Alanons does it take to screw in a light bulb?
None! They just sit back and watch it screw itself.
—ANONYMOUS

When we can sit back and watch others do what they need to do, there's a good program! Old-timers do that better than I do. It takes awhile to give up the instilled belief that I know how to do it best, and even though I'm a *recovering* psychotherapist, I still have attacks of knowing what's best.

· ❧ ·

There's nothing like an old dog with a new trick.

Self-pity

*Self-pity in its early stages is as snug as a
feather mattress. Only when it hardens does it
become uncomfortable.*
—MAYA ANGELOU

Self-pity is deceptive. We use it to gather support, and just when it is broken in, it drives
others away. Maybe it's just better to "take our
lumps."

• ❧ •

There are so many of my "disease techniques" that seemed so rational and effective at the time. Then they harden into
concrete blocks around my ankles. Time to
get out the tools and the solution.

Expectations

On relationships . . . I felt that in today's mating market full of women with power jobs, power wardrobes, and power bodies, I was a power failure!
—DIANE C., *The Mating Manual*

We are always trying to make ourselves into what others think we should be. I call this the "girdle syndrome"—just show me the girdle and I'll try to fit myself into it (even if it is two sizes too small!).

· ✦ ·

Whether I girdle myself into others' expectations or my expectations, they're still expectations. Even an expectation to give up an expectation is an expectation.

Equal Opportunities

Addictions are equal-opportunity diseases.
—HARVEY MILKMAN

What a way to deal with sexism, racism, ageism, classism, and homophobia—anyone can get these diseases. All the "isms" are equal-opportunity. After all, nothing is all bad.

· ✻ ·

Try as we might, we still don't have vaccinations for addictions. Lots of people are offering fixes, though.

Threats

I'm so mad, I won't tell you how I feel.
—ANONYMOUS

Let 'em *beg* to find out that you're mad. That'll teach 'em. When people are willing to work to find out what's going on with you, it proves they love you, right? If we collect enough injustice coupons, we can trade them in on a failed relationship. Then we can take our injustice collection of ruptured relationships on tour—or to a Twelve-Step group if we're lucky.

· 🌿 ·

One of the ways to punish those we love is to withhold our feelings from them. Unfortunately it always works.

Sponsor

We keep a list of "perfect" sponsors in our office for those who have trouble finding one. It's that blank piece of paper on the bulletin board.

—ANONYMOUS

The "search for the perfect sponsor" has allowed many of us to avoid working our program. When we first started attending meetings, it was amazing how obvious the character defects of others were. We secretly wanted someone with great experience who had no character defects. As our recovery progresses, it is amazing how much better people who come to meetings look.

· ❧ ·

Judgmentalism is part of my disease. Letting go of it is part of my recovery.

Hitting Bottom

To be beat is to be at the bottom of your
personality, looking up. —JOHN C. HOLMES

When we are at the bottom looking up, there's no better place to start. At least we don't have to worry about directionality.

• 🌿 •

I prefer not to be confused with complexity. Starting from the bottom is pretty simple.

Staying Stuck

I have all these things I want to do, but I never start doing any of them because I wouldn't have time to do the others.

—OTTO

M y addictions are masters in keeping me stuck. I can invent the most imaginative schemes to do nothing. Yet when I'm doing nothing, I can't do anything.

· 业 ·

If I do what I need to do, I can't do what I want to do. Yet what I want to do doesn't seem as important as what I need to do. Sooo . . . I'd better do nothing.

Avoidance

I do not approach life as a problem to be solved. I approach life as a problem to be avoided.
— BETTY

If life is a problem to be avoided, addictions are a perfect solution.

· ❧ ·

If I avoid my life, who will live it for me? So far, I haven't been impressed with the volunteers.

Holidays

Valentine's Day is to the relationship addict what New Year's Eve is to the alcoholic.

—AWS

I had a client once who complained that he and his wife didn't even have sex on "sexual holidays." Finding no point of reference in myself for this statement, I asked him what he meant by "sexual holidays." He said, "You know, Christmas, Thanksgiving, New Year's, vacations, etcetera."

How often we have associated holidays with various forms of addiction, and have used them to justify or practice our addictions!

· ❧ ·

Holidays look different when I'm sober.

Loving

I used to want to meld with someone. Now I won't settle for all those alloys. I want allies.
—AWS

Funny how our perceptions change. When we are in our disease, our perceptions become distorted by the disease. Addicts are always fixated on swallowing, and love gets equated with being swallowed up by someone. Remember, when something is digested, it is broken up into lots of little pieces.

· 🌿 ·

Take a little love from a lot of people.

Victim

There are no victims, just volunteers.
— DEAN C., AS QUOTED IN *Recovering*

"Bad things do happen to good people." Yet the one way we have to reclaim our power is to take ownership of our lives and quit focusing all of our power on others.

I am advanced in victim skills. I am a neophyte in self-empowerment—the training opportunities seem to be more limited.

One thing I can do is to take ownership of my life and quit volunteering for victim.

· ✖ ·

I know how to do victim, but even a successful victim is a failure.

Letting Go

There are two kinds of people: those who say to God, "Thy will be done," and those to whom God says, "All right, then, have it your way."

—C. S. Lewis

One thing about God, we sure get permission to do it our way. For some of us, having it our way is the only way to get to, "Thy will be done."

· ❧ ·

Having it "our own way" isn't winning.

Recovery as Paradigm Shift

When speaking on the concept of paradigm or systems shift to a group of businessmen recently, I asked them how they felt about the possibility that a loose conglomerate of recovering addicts were the ones leading all of us into the new paradigm. They didn't get the joke.

—AWS

We have been led into many current messes by a group of active addicts. Why is it so surprising that recovering addicts may lead us out of it? They, at least, know the trail.

· 🌿 ·

Trails are better walked by those who made them.

Sponsor

On Jimmy Swaggart confessing to an "unspecified sin"—doesn't he know you're not supposed to do a Fourth or Fifth Step without a sponsor?
                                    —JOHN PAUL COOKLEY

Addictions are tricky diseases. We will always try to get away with whatever we can—or can't.

· ❧ ·

The Twelve Steps would probably be *easier* without a sponsor, and we like "easy" a lot. Easy means getting by, not going through. Tough sponsors make life easier.

Getting "Easy"

It is easier to stay out than to get out.
—MARK TWAIN

E ver tried to get out of an addiction lately? When we were slipping into our addiction, it seemed so easy, so mindless. It hardly took any work at all to become addicted. Maybe that's why we keep looking for a recovery "fix."

· 🌿 ·

Recovery really is simple—it's just not always easy.

Making Changes

The cobwebs in our mind are best cleared with a clean sweep of our life.

—AWS

Brooms may be old-fashioned, and everyone's life needs tidying up occasionally. When I am in my disease, I operate more like a vacuum cleaner sucking up everything in sight. At least brooms allow me the time to pick and choose the areas for cleaning, and they require some "elbow grease" from me.

· ❧ ·

Now, as I tidy up my life, I need to do more than just move the dust around. I need to be willing to go to any lengths.

Ownership

Tongue often hang man quicker than rope.
—CHARLIE CHAN

Being in recovery means that we take as much responsibility (ownership) for what comes out of our mouths as we do for what goes in. The process of recovery is one of progressively owning our lives.

· ☙ ·

Addicts often have big mouths, which are rarely connected with their brains.

Living the Question

I can't say that I have done too well in figuring out all the answers about sobriety, but I have done a sterling job of generating questions!

—AWS

Perhaps that's what sobriety is—generating questions and not having to have the answers.

• ❧ •

Addicts need answers. The process of sobriety is living the questions.

Focusing on Others

Nothing so needs reforming as other people's habits.
                                                —MARK TWAIN

It's so easy to see what others need to do for their recovery. Unfortunately, none of us ever get better from working someone else's program.

• ❧ •

Working on myself is probably more than enough to keep me busy.

Acceptance—Progress

When folks asked me to imagine an animal I would like to be, I always imagined a magnificent black stallion, a powerful lion, or a fleet-footed deer. However, my recovering self seems best characterized by a skinny green inchworm.

—AWS

So much for grandiosity and grand illusions. The glorious leaps of the gazelle and the swift movements of the powerful steed are beautiful, and yet recovery can only happen one step at a time—one day at a time.

· 🌿 ·

Frankly, inching along is probably just about all I can handle right now.

Getting Smart

SIX-YEAR-OLD 1: *Did you see the condom on the patio?*

SIX-YEAR-OLD 2: *What's a patio?*

—ANONYMOUS

We get worldwise early. That doesn't mean we get smart early. In fact, getting smart takes work. It's difficult to get smart when we are playing with a short deck, and our addictions give us a short deck.

Luckily recovery can deal us an ace in the hole, and we can go on from there.

· ☙ ·

In recovery we still may lose a hand or two, but our odds are better.

Entry-Level Positions

In many of my recovery groups there's always
a mad rush for the bottom rung of the ladder.
—AWS

E ven if we're competing to be on the bottom, we compete. Competition feels essential when we don't believe we are enough, and then even a solid slot at the bottom is comforting, if not satisfying. At least no one can push us down any farther.

· 🌿 ·

Sometimes we just make no sense at all. That's an addiction, isn't it?

Higher Power—Step Two

I used to be very skeptical of the need to recognize a Higher Power. However, after careful consideration I realized that I, in fact, wasn't really doing that well on my own.

—ANONYMOUS

How arrogant we become when we have this addictive disease. We really believe that we can make it with no help from anyone or anything. Clearly anyone can see by looking at us that we are doing just fine.

· ❧ ·

If I recognize my need for a Higher Power, then I have to recognize that I'm not a Higher Power. Are there other choices?

Judgmentalism

When I first started attending Twelve-Step meetings, I would secretly sneer when I heard someone say that they were "grateful alcoholics" (codependents, food addicts, workaholics, etc.). Deep inside I believed that notion was proof positive of just how sick they really were.

—AWS

Early in recovery, we see people laugh at things that just hold no humor for us and even seem downright insulting (like calling oneself an "old drunk" or an "old pervert"). When we progress in our recovery, we can see how humorous we were in our "con."

· 🌿 ·

Hindsight may not be so much better than foresight, but it's much better than no sight at all.

March

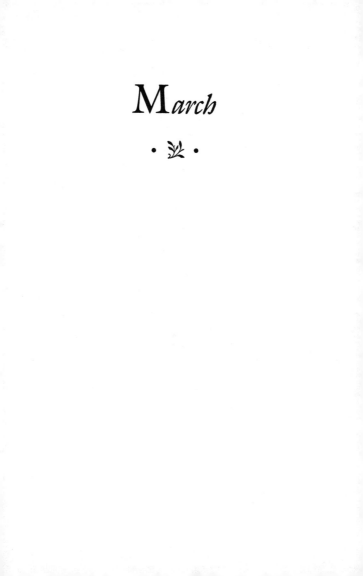

Losses

You can lose a lot on a drinking-man's diet: your liver, weekends, and your driver's license, to mention a few.
—ROBERT ORBEN

Not only can I lose the things I had on a drinking diet, I can brood over losing things I don't have. Then while I'm brooding over the things I don't have, I need a little something to take the edge off, so I can really apply myself to the task at hand—my favorite addiction perhaps.

· ❧ ·

It's always more difficult to lose something we never had.

Asking for Help

Asking for help is a weakness and is only for those who can't make it on their own, right?
—AWS

It's hard to accept help. We addicts are suspicious of help, as well we might be, especially if it's "helpful." Nothing is more fraught with dangers than unsolicited help! On the other hand, it's sure important to reach out and ask for help when we need it.

· 🌿 ·

"The Lord helps those who help themselves"—and sometimes we have to ask first.

Happiness

I ran screaming out of the Venice (California) meeting one night saying, "You sons-a-bitches will never pressure me into happiness." I didn't realize I was already into heavy doses of it.

—SAM MEIER (SERENITY SAM)

We always hear about how difficult recovery is, but usually we hear about the difficulty of recovery from those who haven't tried it or from those who are very early into it. Try it—you'll like it.

• 🌿 •

Recovery can be terrifying. It's an unknown—it's being alive. Good heavens! What am I getting myself into?

Denial

*Some people can't see the trees for the forest,
and some people can't see the forest for the
trees. When I am in my disease, I do a
mighty fine job of clear-cutting it all.*

—AWS

This disease is massive. It is one of life's "clear-cuts." We don't know what we aren't seeing because we can't see it. Denial is everywhere. It clear-cuts reality.

. ⚘ .

Glasses don't help when I don't have my eyes open.

Humility

When I finally hit bottom and called AA, the person on the other end said, "Do you want me to come and get you?" and being about as humble as Hitler, I said, "I'll get there under my own steam."
—DAVID ORONOFSKY

I don't know what all this talk about humility is all about. I'm as humble as the next guy, probably even more so.

· 🌿 ·

When I'm on my knees, it's difficult to look *down* on anyone.

Recovery Process

I knew one woman who got real serious about the Twelve-Step program. She was going to sit down and work through all Twelve Steps in a month and move on. She never moved on.

—AWS

Often we forget that recovery is a process, not a task to be completed. We believe that if we could just get our recovery completed, we could get on with life.

· ✿ ·

We forget that recovery *is* life.

Distractibility

When you're up to your neck in alligators, it's hard to remember you were going to drain the swamp.

—ROSIE ROCCO

Addictions are "busy" diseases. They are jealous lovers. They distract us from ourselves, our work, our families, our friends, and our creativity. That's what we want, isn't it—to be distracted? My what big teeth you have!

· 🌿 ·

Why can't we keep our focus on the job? Because our disease is like being surrounded by alligators. That's why.

"Shoulding."

Don't let people should all over you.
—JOE CRUSE

Ah, yes, "the tyranny of the should." How familiar it is to all of us! When we spend our lives "shoulding," we just get the crust and not the pudding.

· 🌿 ·

You *shouldn't* let it (whatever "it" is) worry you.

Looking "Out There"

I used to wonder where that old saying "Stubborn as a mule" came from. Then I discovered that my partner had a little mule in his/her background.
—ANONYMOUS

I t's easy to see in others those things we refuse to see in ourselves. Well, at least I get credit for surrounding myself with teachers. And I might ask myself what it says about me, if I chose a jackass for a partner.

· 🌿 ·

When I focus on what's wrong with my "teachers," I miss the lessons I can learn from them. It's important to remember that I interviewed them for the job.

Attraction

Believe those who are seeking the truth; doubt those who have found it.
—André Gide

The Twelve Steps of the Alcoholics Anonymous Program is one of attraction and not promotion. It has worked for many of us though it may not work for some. What keeps the program alive is pilgrims, not evangelists.

• ❧ •

When I think I have found the truth, I quit looking.

Procrastination

One of the ways I practice my disease is that I can get distracted by anything, even reading a bean-can label.

—HAROLD

Creative procrastination is one of the skills of the workaholic. The chemical addict isn't the only one who protects her/his supply. Distraction can protect procrastination.

• •

When I am distracted by my procrastination, my workaholism is safe.

Gratitude

I can't imagine where I would be today without my Twelve-Step program. Come to think of it, I can imagine, but I'd rather not.
—ANONYMOUS

The program has helped many of us out of the gutter, whether it be a physical gutter or an emotional gutter—both are hard to crawl out of.

The fellowship, the Steps, and the support of our Higher Power have provided us with the tools of recovery.

· 🌿 ·

When I think of where I might be, I sure am proud to be where I am.

Higher Power

People in the program tell me to trust my Higher Power, but how come I got assigned a Higher Power that takes long vacations and works a short day?

—AWS

Where were you when I needed you? Sometimes I wonder if my Higher Power has taken an early retirement. He/she/it certainly doesn't seem to be in my hire.

One of the things that we learn in recovery is that our Higher Power is not under our control. My Higher Power's *delay* is not denial.

· 🌿 ·

I'm glad my Higher Power isn't under my control. How could I trust something that makes the kind of decisions I do?

Denial

I'm not really codependent, but I have spent a lot of time trying to fix my husband's codependence.
—DEBRA

Whoever heard of a person who isn't a codependent trying to fix someone else's codependence? Aren't we cute? Who said this disease isn't funny? And creative? And . . . maybe I can help them see the error of their ways.

• ❧ •

When I am sure I can help someone see their disease, I'm in *my* disease.

Making Amends—Control

My amends-making got easier when I stopped trying to extract forgiveness from everyone to whom I was making an amend.
　　　　　　　　　　　　　　　　—AWS

Old character defects die hard! The illusion of control is one of the stickiest. Whaddya expect? Making amends and giving up my controlling behavior at the same time? I thought this was a one-step-at-a-time program.

· 🌿 ·

When I remember that amends are made for myself, it's easier for me to let others do what they will with them. See, letting go is really not a control issue, it's a memory issue, and we addicts do have memory problems.

Following My Path

How can my mom make my road map when her road is so wide she weaves all over it?
—ANONYMOUS

When others are trying to tell us how to live our lives, that's a sure sign of their disease. When we listen, it's a sure sign of our disease.

· 🌿 ·

I may need to weave all over my path, but at least it's *my* path.

Living Life

I'm real afraid of dying. Then I guess that
I'm even more afraid of living.
—SUSAN

When we admit we are afraid of living, we are taking a step toward doing it. Even a little honesty goes a long way in this recovery business. Remember, none of us will get out of this life alive.

· 🌿 ·

It's okay to be scared!

Suffering

Pain is unavoidable, suffering is optional.
—DEAN C., AS QUOTED IN *Recovering*

Some of the black folks in the ghettos are teaching us this when they personally take stands to rid their communities of drugs. Suffering isn't romantic, and giving it up isn't either. Doing something about our lives opens doors to new possibilities. We can learn something from them.

• ☙ •

If I let myself hurt when I hurt, I probably won't have to suffer so much.

Losing Ourselves, Having Ourselves

I'm always worrying about losing myself but I suddenly realized—not to worry—how can I lose something I don't have?

—AWS

We addicts spend a lot of time protecting ourselves and trying to hold on to ourselves.

• ❧ •

Ironically when we *have* ourselves, we don't worry about *losing* ourselves.

Savoring the World

I arise in the morning torn between a desire to improve (or save) the world and a desire to enjoy (or savor) the world. This makes it hard to plan the day.
—E. B. WHITE

Please save us from those who want to save us. And save us from our desire to save others. And save us from trying to save us from those who want to save us . . . and . . .

· 🌱 ·

Savoring my day may be the only way to save myself or anyone else.

Logical, Rational Nonsense

Pat Robertson took credit for turning away Hurricane Gloria from the beach. Maybe we should all start taking credit for things that didn't happen.
—JOHN PAUL COOKLEY

I've heard tell that if we just hold our breath every morning and then say, "Tiger away, tiger away," it keeps tigers from coming around. It must work—I've been doing it for fifteen years and haven't seen a tiger yet.

· 🌱 ·

Some thinking is rational and logical—it just doesn't make any sense.

Dependency

One codependent to another, "Do you think it's all right to lend your codependence books?"
—KATE CLINTON

We codependents never know what to do, and we want to do the "right" thing. We also want to be helpful, kind, caring, and useful. Why is that so bad? If we have to ask the question, we probably won't understand the answer.

· 🌿 ·

When I need someone else to tell me what's right, I am probably not prepared to hear what they say.

Insanity

*We should be careful to get out of an
experience only the wisdom that is in it—and
stop there; lest we be like the cat that sits
down on a hot stove lid. She will never sit
down on a hot stove lid again, and that is
well; but also she will never sit down on a cold
one anymore.*
— MARK TWAIN

Addicts tend to view the world in a peculiar idiosyncratic way. We often draw conclusions that only make sense to a confused mind. . . . It's called "stinkin' thinkin' "!

· 🌱 ·

"Insanity" may well be getting the wrong
wisdom from the "right" experience.

Power Greater Than Ourselves

It takes a very rainy day to drown a duck.
—CHARLIE CHAN

Surprisingly, by the grace of our power greater than ourselves, we have avoided drowning ourselves. We may have been busily treading water, and without our knowing it, we seemed to have had some invisible Higher Power water wings.

· ⚘ ·

When we are swimming in our disease, we need all the help we can get—webbed feet, gills, you name it, I'll take it.

Control

*And then she said to me with great
tenderness, "Just remember, honey, a
caterpillar is not in charge of becoming a
butterfly."*
—Anonymous

If only I could keep things under *control*! I
think I could make an excellent H.P. assistant. I'm humble. I don't have to have the top job
(although that would be nice); an assistant will do
just fine. At least I'd have access to the top.

· 🌿 ·

If I am going to "emerge" and become a
butterfly, I feel that I am at least entitled to
choose the colors! (Come to think of it,
wing shape and size would be nice, too.)

Living Sober

*Getting sober's not the problem. It's the living
sober that's difficult.*

—AWS

I have quit my addiction a million times—big
deal. We addicts like to experiment and we
are happy to "experiment" with sobriety. But living honestly, clearly, fully, and presently does,
however, offer a challenge.

· 🌿 ·

When I experiment with my sobriety, I
may blow up the laboratory of my life.

Self-Esteem

When we see a person with tire tracks across their chest, we realize that they are the kind that will volunteer for a job as a speed bump.
—CHARLES WHITFIELD

Sometimes it is difficult for us to see that we hold ourselves in such low esteem that we are not only willing to let others walk over us, we are willing to let them drive over us. If corrugated roads were still being built, we would honor ourselves by volunteering to be a log.

· 🌿 ·

It's really hard to see tire marks on our own chest when we keep focusing our attention "out there."

Normal

*My family was so dysfunctional that I thought
that yelling, screaming, hitting each other,
and hiding in the closet were normal.*
—TERRY KELLOG

One of the effects of this disease is that we
gradually lose our ability to see insanity
and remember clarity. In fact, if we grew up in
severely dysfunctional families, we may have no
basis for determining sanity.

· ☙ ·

This addictive disease may be the norm,
but it isn't normal.

Knowing Why

My "whying" has certainly fed into my dying.
—MARYLU

I just want to know *why*. *Why* do I have this disease? *Why* don't I get better? Why do *I* have to work so hard at recovery? Why do others have it easier? (pant, pant)

Somehow we believe if we can just *understand,* everything will be better. Information is important, and no one ever recovers from understanding.

· ❧ ·

Recovery is a process. I am a process. There is no "quick fix" for me or my recovery.

Disease—Step One

Some people complain that Twelve-Step jokes are sick humor. Why not? We're sick, aren't we?

—ANONYMOUS

B ig deal! I have a disease shared by millions! Where are the sober role models? Where are those *not* like me? How can I possibly get better if I surround myself with "sickies" like me?

• ❧ •

Today I will open myself to the possibility (however remote) of being grateful for my disease and for my companions in recovery. Yet, how can one be grateful for something that's so "common"?

Saying No

I think we should start a book club for codependents. No one would have the option of saying no to any selection.
—TOM GRADY

Recovery is much more complex than "just saying no." As codependents we also realize that saying no, even when it is in our best interest, is not always easy. In early recovery we often say no even when we do not need to, just for practice.

Let me know today the noes that are mine and give me the wisdom to know how to say them. Most of all, let me not buy any books that I don't really want.

April

Cosmic Mate

*When I was on the search for the cosmic mate,
I tended to exclude people like myself.*

—AWS

Funny how looking for a mate works. Likes don't really attract, they repel. At least at first glance. What I usually choose in my addictive disease are people who don't threaten my addictive process.

· 🌿 ·

Until I get clearer, I'd better not choose to try to be intimate with people like me.

Creative Avoidance

The process of life didn't interest me, the goal of enlightenment did. I was willing to turn in peace and happiness right now for the promise of enlightenment in the future.
—MICHELE L., AS QUOTED IN *Recovering*

One thing about addicts—we are creative. We are very inventive at ways of getting out of living our lives, while looking like we're sincere and even, perhaps, like we're doing it (life that is). Nobody ever said we were dumb.

· 🌿 ·

If I put the energy into recovery that I have put into creative avoidance, I would be one of the "old-timers."

Recovery—Hitting Bottom

The elevator goes to the bottom, but you can get off at any floor.

—Anonymous

Addicts don't want to miss anything. If we don't hit bottom, how can we have the full experience of this disease?

· 🌿 ·

Maybe there's an "easier, softer" bottom—addicts are sure dedicated to trying to find it.

Being Human

I'm uncomfortable with perfect. I don't trust people who don't have mental breakdowns on a regular basis.
                              —SAM MEIER (SERENITY SAM)

When I resist being human, I have to be a phony. If I'm phony, I'm not who I am. If I'm not who I am, I can't be perfectly who I am.

• ❧ •

The only *real* problem with being human is trying not to be.

Escaping

*Sometimes I wish I could be someone else.
Then I realize, the only thing I haven't tried
is being myself.*
—AWS

E scape! Get out! I don't want to be doing
this. Please don't make me do this. Living
my *own* life is just too much to ask.

• ⚘ •

Try it. You'll like it.

Approval

*I have lived my life around the motto
"Approval at any cost"—and it has cost a
lot!*
—JUDY

G iving up "me" to have people like me
doesn't really result in my "me" being there
to be liked, does it? Right on! The stakes are
pretty high.

· ※ ·

Approval can never come from outside.
Even when others want to give it, they just
do not have it to give. Whether they know
this or not is not our problem.

Relationships

I married this wonderful woman and she didn't realize that she was marrying an alcoholic. And we didn't start to build a marriage, we started to build a booby trap, one that could go off any year.

—DAVID ORONOFSKY

It looks like we're doing the right thing—we're certainly doing what we know best. Unfortunately we may be skilled as an addict, but those skills don't transfer to living life.

· ✹ ·

What's wrong with using control, dishonesty, entrapment, and manipulation to form relationships? It's what my parents did.

Geographic Cure

Wherever you go, there you are.

—Kermit the Frog

The old geographic cure—seems like it should work. New place, new scenery, new set of friends, new love. Unfortunately I have to take me with me.

• ❧ •

Even when I leave me, I'm still there.

Learnings, Arrogance

I have learned (painfully, I might add) that the tuition I have to pay for each new learning is directly proportionate to my level of stubbornness (denial, resistance, defensiveness). The greater the resistance, the higher the tuition.

—AWS

There don't seem to be any scholarships in the University of Life. I set the tuition myself, and when I hold on to my arrogance and stubbornness, it gets pretty high.

• ❧ •

I'm working full-time to pay the tuition I have set up for life's learnings.

Gluttony

You can't have everything—where would you put it?
—ANONYMOUS

G luttony is part of the disease of addiction. When I am into my disease, I can never get enough of anything. There just isn't enough to fill my need because my addictions never fill my needs. I really don't want to have everything, but . . . a little more (and then a little more . . . and then a little more) would be nice.

My Higher Power helps me see that enough is often less than the "more" I thought I needed.

Stubborn

I used to think I was tenacious and dedicated until I discovered the word stubborn.

—AWS

Why is it that since I have started my recovery, all my assets have turned into liabilities? I don't know. Could it be something about screwed-up perception?

· ❧ ·

As I change, my perceptions change.

Self-pity

Self-pity is easily the most destructive of the nonpharmaceutical narcotics; it is addictive, gives momentary pleasure, and separates the victim from reality.
—JOHN W. GARDNER

I just thought of a good money-maker. Disposable, folding, traveling pity-pots. I'll bet I could make a mint. I knew there was money in addictions.

• ✣ •

It isn't destructive to feel sorry for ourselves; it's destructive to stay stuck in feeling sorry for ourselves.

Fixes

I started getting better when I got out of the self-help section.
—DAVE

Fixes come in many forms. One of the ways of protecting our supply is sincerely embracing a variety of quick fixes. Self-help books are so popular because they protect our supply. We feel instantly better and we don't disturb our addictions. A rule of thumb—if it's quick and easy, it ain't recovery.

· ✹ ·

Real self-help can't come from outside. A partnership between myself and my Higher Power is the help I need.

Gifts

When I'm like my mother, I know it's time to go to treatment.

—ANONYMOUS

Often it is the trouble spots in our life that get us where we need to be. Our gifts come in strange packages. Whatever works. Whatever gets us there!

· 🌿 ·

When I am having a big trouble with someone, it's a sure sign that person is exactly the gift I am needing in my life. Sometimes it takes me years to write the thank-you note, though.

One Step at a Time

You seem real clear—clearly confused.

—AWS

One step at a time is all we need—if we are clear that we are confused. That's one step away from total confusion. Out of acknowledgment of confusion comes clarity; out of acknowledgment of powerlessness comes strength. Confusing but true! We don't need to make sense of this program for it to work.

· 🌿 ·

If I take one step at a time, pretty soon I find that I am walking the walk. Talking the talk's not so important.

Letting Go

In my life I was either swinging or ducking.
—Susan

When we are either swinging or ducking, we are stuck in our dualistic functioning and lose the possibilities of options. When we lose options, we lose life.

• 🌿 •

Recovery presents us with the option of giving up both ends of any dualism and choosing the third option, which may be flying by the seat of our pants. If we thought our addictions were exciting, wait until we try flying by the seat of our pants.

Addictive Society

Addiction is the identified patient in a culture of dysfuntion.
—DEAN C., AS QUOTED IN *Recovering*

Heavy burden! We know that "identified patients" in families—the ones seen as sick—carry the burden for the disease of the family system. Are we, as addicts, willing to carry the burden for an addicted society? No medals for this one.

· ✣ ·

If we keep looking for the chicken and the egg, we fail to notice that the henhouse is burning down.

Care-aholic

You're clearly a relationship addict when you call the suicide-prevention hot line, get miffed at the counselor for putting religious garbage on you, hang up—and then call back to apologize and see if she's okay. —CAROL

I wish I could just once be okay about my feelings. Why do I feel that my feelings are not legitimate and not okay? Maybe because I have heard that so much.

Being a relationship addict is not genetic. We have had to have careful tutoring to learn that others' feelings are more important than our own and to learn to shut off and negate what is going on inside of us.

· ꙮ ·

What's learned can be unlearned.

Our Bodies

What are you laughing about? My body is a pure temple—desperately in need of repair.
—HAL SCHIPPITS

Our bodies are temples and we have battered them terribly. Recovery means attending to and repairing our bodies. We have not respected our bodies because we have not respected ourselves. We have paid the wrecking crew, now how about some funds for the remodelers?

· 🌿 ·

My disease operates on many levels. My recovery operates on many levels. Let's hope they're the same levels.

Following a Con

I have noted that persons with bad judgment are most insistent that we do what they think best.
— LIONEL ABEL

Remember, the one who pushes the hardest and cons the best may be someone who hasn't started recovery yet.

· 🌿 ·

Only fools would be led by fools—and these types do not seem to be in short supply.

Denial

For the longest time I never believed I was an alcoholic. I was so into denial I convinced myself that I was a stunt man for Cutty Sark.
—JOHN PAUL COOKLEY

Ain't denial wonderful? It helps us take the truth and make it confusing. The problem is, I don't know when I'm denying my denial.

· 🌿 ·

Denying my denial is a personal betrayal.

Being Noisy

Noise proves nothing. Often a hen who has merely laid an egg cackles as if she has laid an asteroid.
—MARK TWAIN

Cackling hens are announcing their eggs. Cackling addicts are announcing their disease. When we are uncertain about ourselves, we usually "announce" ourselves with great fanfare.

· 🌿 ·

The more our recovery progresses, the quieter we seem to get.

Memory

How do you expect me to learn from my past
when I have no memory?

—AWS

Learning has not been my strong suit for
these last few diseased years. Yet recovery
has offered me the opportunity to learn from
everything—my successes, my failures, my mistakes, and my life—nothing is irrelevant.

· ❧ ·

I hope I can remember not to forget that
I *can* remember.

The Rat Race

The trouble with the rat race is that even if you win, you're still a rat.
—LILY TOMLIN

Sadly many of us entered a race where winning was losing. Who really wants to be the best addict around? Recovery helps us to see that both the rat and the race are irrelevant.

• ❧ •

Sprinting for recovery is much better than lolling in the abyss of the disease, but let's make sure we are in the right race before we leave the starting block.

Procrastination

After all is said and done, more is said than done.
—Anonymous

Procrastination isn't limited to addicts, but we clearly have learned to do it with a certain flair. Talent is great, but a talented procrastinator? Why not? It takes all kinds. I always admire excellence wherever I see it. That doesn't mean I choose to hang around it, though.

· 🌿 ·

We are often so busy being busy that we don't realize that if we quit being so busy, we might get something done.

Invisibility

I try to be invisible until I'm seen.
—NANCY E.S.

Now, there's a good one! Remember when we were kids, how we believed that no one could see us when we held our hands over our eyes?

For the addict, hiding becomes a way of life. We try to isolate and become invisible and we wait for others to take the initiative and the responsibility. If someone reaches out to us, we might be willing to let them.

· ✺ ·

We know how *not* to be there. How about being there?

Trusting the Process

Don't try to be a saint before next Thursday!
—BILL W.

Getting to be a worn-out, worn-down addict takes time. Most of us have not lost our morality, our integrity, and our concern for others overnight. We have had to work at it over a number of years. Sometimes we fail to recognize the time and effort that we gave to our addiction. We have to admit that there was a certain devotion present.

· ❧ ·

What makes us think that becoming a saint will take less time than it took us to become a poorly functioning addict?

Step Two, Step Three, Step Eleven

Even if you can't believe in a God, can you believe you ain't Him?

—CONNIE G.

For some of us, getting past Step Two and Step Three is excruciatingly difficult. We block out God—Him. We block out God, period.

We sense some forces in the universe greater than ourselves and yet we struggle with childhood images and believed betrayals. We long for something greater than ourselves, yet part of our disease is a loss of trust and an increasing self-centeredness.

• ⚜ •

Well, I suppose it's a start to *come* to believe that whatever there is out there greater than myself, I ain't it.

Cons—Blind Spots

At meetings I have often heard people say, "I have one of the best cons around." I wonder where all the mediocre conners are!

—AWS

Addiction is such a creative and fascinating disease. Unfortunately we often face off with one of our favorite character defects while subtly expressing another. Our arrogance is probably just a little more subtle than our con.

My blind spots are just that—blind spots. Recovery works best when our blind spots don't coincide and overlap with those of our friends.

• 🌿 •

Before I became humble, I was blind to my arrogance. I'm so glad that all that's changed.

Recovery—Bullshit

What do you call a person who is addicted to milk?
A cow-dependent.

—Gwen DeCino

• 🌿 •

We are so fortunate to be living in a time when millions are entering upon recovery from a variety of addictions. We are learning that most of us have multiple expressions for our addictive process and that regardless of what our addictions are, recovery *is* possible. When we can joke among ourselves and with ourselves, we know that the recovery process is happening.

• 🌿 •

I would rather admit that I am a cow-dependent than continue with my bullshit.

May

Chains That Bind

I have heard it said that the chains that bind you are too strong to break by the time you know they are there.

—Diane C., as quoted in *Recovering*

We don't always see too clearly. Perhaps that's why we need the support of a fellowship and a power greater than ourselves. As we listen to others share their stories and their struggles, we learn about ourselves.

Why didn't I realize that I needed to listen to other addicts to learn about myself? Because you're an addict, that's why.

Memory

I've been sober four years, six months, two weeks, three days, and eleven minutes, but I don't think about it at all.

—QUOTED BY BILL BROOKS

S trange, as we get sober, we seem to remember what's important. Before we started getting sober, we didn't remember anything at all.

· 🌿 ·

If I focus on the fine details, maybe the big things will take care of themselves.

Illusion of Security

I'm a professional balker. I'm very afraid of change. I'm the type of person that if I fall into a rut, I'll start hanging pictures, move in, and make it a home.

—SAM MEIER (SERENITY SAM)

Ah, the illusion of security. We have come to equate security and stasis. The only thing that is completely still is a dead person, and even she/he is decaying.

· ✲ ·

Security is not outside. It's inside.

Confusion

We addicts sometimes forget what's important. Of course it's difficult to forget what's important when we never knew.

—AWS

Our disease is a perceptual disease. We have trouble distinguishing between figure and ground. Often we don't know what *is* figure and ground. Everything becomes important, and nothing is. Gets confusing, doesn't it?

• ✾ •

If I don't know what's important, I don't have to deal with anything—Right?

Let Go

As said by his sponsor: "There are thousands who have come to Alcoholics Anonymous who have tried to change that book (Alcoholics Anonymous). *The key is, David, let that book change you."*
—DAVID ORONOFSKY

Can we run the risk of letting something that isn't perfect (not with the *right* language and *right* ideas) influence us? The question is, Can we afford *not* to take the risk?

· 𝕩 ·

Take what you need and leave the rest.

Logic

If the right brain controls the left side of the body and the left brain controls the right side of the body, then it can, therefore, safely be assumed that only left-handed people are in their right minds.

—ANONYMOUS

O ften I sound logical but I don't make any sense. Logic is frequently a mask for confusion or a generator of confusion.

· 🌿 ·

When I am right with myself, I don't have to worry which side of my brain I'm in.

A Self Program

Recovery can be like . . . a ship leaving sinking rats.
—JOHN BENNETT, VIA JOHN CASTEEL

Some of those "rats" we're deserting are our family and best friends! We can't do our recovery for or against those in our life. If we are willing to put our sobriety first, we have to be *willing* to let anything go.

· ※ ·

Recovery has to be for ourselves. If my recovery isn't for me, it's not recovery!

Lying—Common Denominators

We may call them white lies, little lies, harmless lies, or unimportant lies, but the one thing they have in common is that they are all lies.

—AWS

Sometimes, in our quest for variety (commonly called rationalization), we fail to see the common denominator. Often the common denominator is our disease. When we see our disease as the common denominator, we can then begin to look at specifics.

· 🌱 ·

Having a million ways of lying is not really a good use for our creativity.

Accepting All of Ourselves

Everyone is born a genius, but the process of living de-geniuses them.

—R. BUCKMINSTER FULLER

Sometimes I feel the faint traces of my old genius self, but who needs the wisdom of a six-month-old? We all do!

· 🌿 ·

For all of us there was a time . . . maybe way back, when we were in touch with our own wisdom. That can happen again.

Conning

*The important thing about a clearness con
is that one is always muddled when she/he
uses it.*
                                                    —AWS

One of the things that I love about this disease is that it offers endless possibilities for
learning and it is so cunning, baffling, powerful,
and patient that it offers a lifetime of challenges.
When we use "being clear" to cover up the fact
that we aren't, we're slipperier than an eel on ice
skates.

· 🌿 ·

One of the ways I'm slippery is in trying to
look like I'm not.

Procrastination

I'm good at what I do, but I seldom do it.
—HAROLD

True work addicts are often good at what they do and they often spend more time avoiding work than doing it. Work addicts work hard at procrastination. After all, it takes a great deal of creativity *not* to do things we're good at.

• ❧ •

Maybe I'm also good at what I *do do,* which is *not doing it.* (Whatever *it* is!)

Trust

I do trust my Higher Power with all my heart and soul—not without fear. I would still like to have a forty-day notice of what's going to happen in my life.

—JUDY

Trust is never easy for an addict. Trusting a Higher Power when we haven't been keeping up our end of the communication is even tougher. Trusting with qualifications is a start.

· ❧ ·

Sometimes one-half a step at a time looks real big.

Crisis

I am in a healthy relationship now. I used to call that boredom.
—Susan

A crisis a moment, that's what relationships used to be. It's funny how perceptions change. As we recover, it's difficult to rev up a crisis, no matter how much we try.

· ✌ ·

Recovery is when crisis changes from being exciting, to being exhausting, to being irrelevant.

Being Right

I spent so many years being right that I didn't have the time to notice that my rightness was wrong for me.

—AWS

Sometimes we get so focused on being right that it doesn't even matter what the issue is, we have to be right about it. Sometimes we even *forget* what the issue is. Our rightness is often wrong for us, but we are so invested in the righteousness of wrongness that we don't see that wrongness may be more right for us at that moment. Whew!

· 💐 ·

Give me the serenity to understand this meditation for myself today.

Naming the Problem

I hear that addiction is just a case of misplaced responsibility. I know I misplaced it. I just wonder where it can be found.

—SUSAN

When I misplace my responsibility, I do not misplace my accountability and blame. I misplace my ability to respond. Without my ability to respond, I am facing a lost humanity.

· ❧ ·

Sometimes naming the problem does not always provide the solution. It sure is hard to find the solution *without* naming the problem, though.

Gratitude

Better to have bad breath than no breath at all.
—DEAN C., AS QUOTED IN *Recovering*

Everything's relative! As far as I know, it's hard to sober up when we're dead. When we start exploring possibilities for gratitude, it's amazing how many are all around us.

· ❧ ·

Gratitude comes in all kinds of packages.

Excuses

"If the Lord wanted me to touch my toes, He would have given me longer arms or taller toes!"
— Hal Schippits

We addicts always have someone or something "out there" we can make responsible for what's going on "in here." How about looking at ourselves?

· ⚘ ·

Sometimes in recovery it helps to bend my knees.

Living

When childhood dies, its corpses are called adults.
—Brian Aldiss

W hy must we kill our happy, playful beings to become an adult? Who wants to be around an "old poop," anyway? Even "old poops" don't like being around "old poops."

• ❧ •

Living is really the issue, isn't it? A dead childhood is probably the only corpse that can be resurrected if we willingly *step* into the process.

Medication

Tammy Faye Bakker said she was addicted to
asthma medication. That's the first time I
ever heard cocaine called that.

—JOHN PAUL COOKLEY

Sometimes I become truly annoyed by what
falls under the heading of medicinal. Whis-
key and honey become cough syrup. Drugs "take
the edge off." Sugar and coffee "keep us going."
We are ingenious in generating medicinal "cures"
that perpetuate our disease.

· ❧ ·

The real question is, What are we medicat-
ing?

Truth Speaking

When in doubt, tell the truth.

—MARK TWAIN

Just tell the truth. Sounds easy, doesn't it? Our truth is still there; we have just lost touch with it over time. Sometimes in meetings we listen to others search for their truth—and Eureka! we find our own.

· ✿ ·

If we don't know our truth, we can't say it. When we know it, it's easier to show up and speak up.

Gratitude

Not all who would can be psychotic.
—R.D. LAING

Not all who would can be addicts, but most can. Ever heard of a "grateful addict"? Everyone who is in recovery has!

• 🌿 •

Our disease puts us in the darnedest places. Yet, we have to admit, it did push us into recovery.

Self-deception

A con is only as good as the flair with which it's done.
—Anonymous

S elf-deception is the highest form of deception and produces the lowest form of living. Why is it we are *most* effective when deceiving ourselves?

· 🌿 ·

If I'm deceiving myself, how do I know when I'm doing it?

Not Having Time for Recovery

Workaholics Anonymous probably has something to offer me, but I haven't had time to check it out.
—MARI

Before we start recovery, we seem to have so much time for our disease and nothing left for recovery. We don't seem to realize that not having time for healthy living is part of the disease.

· 🌱 ·

Recovery isn't nearly so time-consuming as addictions. It's just less familiar.

Getting Healthy

Of all the nerve. My Higher Power doesn't only want me to get rid of my addiction, it (she, he) wants me to get healthy.

—AWS

Is there no end to this recovery stuff? Do I really have to get honest, move off my self-centeredness, give up perfectionism, take responsibility for myself, loosen my control, and live my own life? What a drag!

• ❧ •

Wanta see a drag? Try being around someone lounging in the disease.

Skills

*I felt real accomplished as an addict (co), but
sobriety requires skills that I either didn't
know existed or thought were liabilities.*

—ANONYMOUS

A ddicts are not without skills. We can create
instant chaos. We can con our way in or out
of anything. And we have raised controlling to an
art. Unfortunately none of these skills is very
relevant to recovery. Learning to tell the truth,
turn it over, and let go are new skills. Whoever
thought we'd see the day when we'd want to do
any of those things?

· 🌿 ·

Times change!

Doing It Hard

This lesson is so easy, I must be doing it wrong.

—Jo L.

If there is anything that we addicts know how to do and know how to do well, it is "hard." We do life hard. It is inconceivable to us that anything worthwhile could be learned if it does not involve deep pain and horrendous suffering. So, we set up our lives accordingly.

After we have been in recovery awhile, we are so amazed when lessons occasionally come easy. Sometimes we miss them because they are not accompanied by a proper brass band and trauma.

· ❧ ·

I will always go through difficult times. Yet I don't have to make them more difficult than they need to be.

Workaholism

*I recently was given a flyer for some new
workaholic Twelve-Step meetings forming in
the San Francisco Bay area. At the bottom, it
said, "If you are too busy to attend these
meetings, we'll understand."*
—ANONYMOUS

It's not always easy to laugh at our disease. Yet
when we do, we almost always feel more
relaxed and ready to face it at a new level. I have
heard it said that workaholism is the addiction of
the unworthy. All of us can relate to that!

When I am taking time for myself, I really
am not taking it away from someone else.

Serenity

*I don't know what's going on with me. I seem
to be numb. I am not feeling upset, angry,
sad, or fearful. Wait a minute—do you think
this is what some "normal" people call
contentment?*

—BARBARA

Addictions are exciting. There is always a
laugh, or a scream, or a horror a minute.

When we start to recover, we often do not
know how to label the new feelings that come up.
The first time we experience serenity, it often zips
through our consciousness like a meteorite and
scares us to death.

· ❧ ·

It takes some doing to be happy, serene,
and content. Maybe I can stand it.

Doing It Hard

*Recovery is not so bad. It's kinda like walking
backward through molasses up to your crotch
with your legs tied together.*
                                        —AWS

O ne of our favorite theme songs is "It's So
   Hard." Actually somewhere in recovery we
begin to recognize that it is not that recovery is
so difficult, it is our disease that makes life so
hard. When we are operating out of our disease,
we do experience a certain amount of stress and
strain. When we get out of life's way, it just seems
to move along.

• ❧ •

Is it possible to live "the good life" if I'm
not suffering? Is the answer my next step
in recovery? Can life really be that easy?

Sobriety

After two years of recovery if I had known then what I know now, I would never have started.
—ANONYMOUS

How fortunate for us that our ability to have a perspective on sobriety increases with our recovery. Truly it is one of the miracles that so many people are starting on the path to recovery when many who have come from dysfunctional families have no experience of what healthy functioning is and few sober role models.

· 🌿 ·

When I don't know where I'm going, it sure is scary to start. But being scared is no stranger to *me*. Getting started is a novelty, though.

Patience

If it is worth doing, it is worth doing wrong until you get it right.
—DEAN C., AS QUOTED IN *Recovering*

It's hard for us to get it right the first time—but we addicts sure *want to*. Patience, little jackass, patience.

Perfectionism and patience are not mutually supportive processes. If we can be patient with our mistakes, we will probably do better.

· 🌿 ·

When I pray for patience, I must remember that I don't have to have it *right now*!

June

Progression of the Disease

The man who views the world at fifty the same as he did at twenty has wasted thirty years of his life.
— Muhammad Ali

Well, there's something positive to be said for addiction. The disease is either moving forward or moving backward. It never stands still. Unfortunately it's usually getting worse.

· 🌿 ·

Nothing is *all* bad.

Recovering Our Memory

One of the reasons we focus upon the difficulties in recovery is because we have little memory of living in our disease.
—AWS

When people tell us how difficult recovery is, I think that we addicts are probably blessed that we have no memory. Of course, what we can't seem to remember is what it was like to live wholely. Listening to others helps us remember ourselves.

· ✢ ·

Recovery is just one damned thing after another. Of course, living in my disease was, too—I just didn't notice it then.

Control, Being Controlled

*This life is a test. If it were real life, we
would be told where to go and what to do.*
— ANONYMOUS

P lease, please just give me a road map. I follow directions well (I try), I do what I'm
told (most of the time), and I'm willing to be
agreeable (if I agree), so, *please,* just tell me how
to do it.

• 🌿 •

There are a lot of folks out there willing to
tell me what to do—but most of them
know nothing about my life and who I am.
Yet if I turn my life over to them, I don't
have to take ownership if things go
wrong—or do I?

Stinkin' Thinkin'

I saw the most dangerous sign you can put in this kind of group—Think—'cause it's dangerous for our kind of folks to think.
—DAVID ORONOFSKY

Ever hear of stinkin' thinkin'? It sounds logical and rational, it just doesn't make any sense—except to an addict. When we realize how common crazy thinking is, we realize what a dangerous sign *Think* is.

• 🌿 •

If we're crazy, it's dangerous for us to think, and if we're not crazy, it's dangerous for us to think. The question is, Dangerous for whom?

"True Love"

She's the kind of woman whose relationship addiction has turned her into a vacuum cleaner. She'll suck up anyone in sight.

—AWS

True love for relationship addicts is swallowing or being swallowed up. How do I know you love me if you don't want to devour me?

• 🌿 •

It's hard to recognize that healthy relationships require separateness when we keep hearing that the two shall become one.

Dependency

A good codependent wakes up and asks her/his partner, "What kind of day am I going to have?"
—ANONYMOUS

G ood codependents always assume that others have more information about them than they have about themselves. Another good codependent is always willing to tell us what kind of day we will have. With friends like these, who needs to think for herself/himself at all?

· ❦ ·

If I take responsibility for myself, who will take care of everyone else?

Society as Addict

*A civilized society is one which tolerates
eccentricity to the point of doubtful sanity.*
— ROBERT FROST

When we recognize that society encourages
and tolerates addictions, and when we realize that to encourage and tolerate addiction is
to be insane, then we can see that not only in-
dividuals and families but also society needs a
greater power that can restore us to sanity.

• 🌿 •

It's hard to be sober when our society is
drunk.

Control

I want instant results and I think I can make them happen.
　　　　　　　　　　　　　　　　—DONNA

Grandiosity is believing that we can *make* things happen. Pseudohumility is believing that things happen *to* us. Reality is taking ownership and trusting the process!

· 🌿 ·

Many of us are stand-up comics who have been sitting down on the job.

Prickly

You could make a porcupine look snuggly.
—Anonymous

I'm sure porcupines look snugly to other porcupines, but I wouldn't want to snuggle up to one. Recovery means learning to respect (at a reasonable distance) people who are prickly.

· 🌿 ·

When relationship addicts see porcupine persons, they believe turning themselves into pincushions is the way to intimacy.

Qualifying Life and Ourselves

*All my life, I think, perhaps, that I have a
little problem with self-confidence . . . maybe.*
—EDELGARD

Sometimes, we try to qualify ourselves right
out of existence. We are so afraid of being
wrong that we end up saying nothing. No skill
should be wasted: Addicts make good politicians.

· 🌿 ·

Qualifiers rarely add quality to our life.

Being in the "Now"

*Beware of the light at the end of the
tunnel—it may be the headlight of an
oncoming train!*
—ROSIE ROCCO

Things aren't always what they *seem* to be.
When we leave the present, we tend to distort the future and worship the past. Right now
is all we have.

· 🌿 ·

Looking for the light at the end of the
tunnel robs us of the experience of the
tunnel.

Recovery

As I am around recovering people, I have less opportunity for the luxury of being in my addictive disease and . . . it pisses me off.
—ANONYMOUS

There are a lot of things that piss us off about recovery. It's okay to be pissed off. At least we're beginning to *feel* something.

· ❧ ·

Beginning to have feelings isn't all bad. We can have feelings of joy, serenity, happiness, and peacefulness too.

Romance Addictions

*I'm totally fascinated with how she looks. We
don't even connect. We can't even talk. I
don't even like her. A perfect setup for
romance addiction.*
—Susan

Romance addiction requires illusions. Illusions run from reality. When I love my
illusions of a person, I don't have to deal with
that person. Romance addictions make relationships so much tidier.

· ※ ·

If we really *liked* the people we were attracted to, maybe we wouldn't foist our
addictions on them.

Tunnel Vision

It took me three years to figure out you could use the Twelve Steps for something other than alcohol.

—ANONYMOUS

Some people *never* figure out that the Twelve-Step program can be used for something other than alcohol. And some people never figure out that they have more than one addiction. One program—endless applications.

· ❧ ·

Tunnel vision is only great in a tunnel.

Perspective—Quitting

*I didn't have a drinking problem. I had a
quitting problem.*
— DEAN C., AS QUOTED IN *Recovering*

It's all in how you look at it. As our perspective
changes, our response changes. And there's
nothing clearer than the perspective of the addict, right?

· ☙ ·

What I need is a little perspective adjust-
ment.

Pain in Relationships

I have two lovely children, and never has one of them said, "I want to go over to Tommy's or Louise's house because they're going to hit me in the head with a board."

—HAL SCHIPPITS

I wonder when we learned that relationships were, by definition, painful.

· ❧ ·

What's learned can be unlearned.

Give Me a Break—Lying

One lie a day keeps sobriety away. —AWS

All I want is a little break. Can't you give me a little break? Can't I just have a little leeway?

You already have!

· 🌿 ·

When I am constantly looking for a break, I may be shattering my life.

Meanness

Fanatic—one who having forgotten the end, multiplies the mean.
—GEORGE SANTAYANA

O ften we addicts hold on to persons, places, and things when a fool would long since have quit. And we get *mean* while doing it.

· ❧ ·

When I am mean, I usually don't mean what I say and I usually say it in a meaning-less way.

Living

All say, "How hard it is that we have to die"—a strange complaint to come from the mouths of people who have had to live.

—MARK TWAIN

We often seem more comfortable with killing ourselves (slowly, perhaps) than we are with facing life. The familiar is always easier.

· 🌿 ·

Let's take a chance on living—before we die!

Acceptance

I used to resent those "dead days" in recovery when it seemed like I made no progress at all. And then I realized that they were like the burps of life. If they hadn't come up, they would have become the "old farts" of my disease.

—AWS

Recovery depends upon the direction that we take. When anything comes up, accept it. Otherwise it may have to get pushed down and get compacted.

Whatever comes up must have been down there.

Gratitude

I am more important than my problems.
—José Ferrer

We can remember times when we found it hard to believe that we were more important than our problems. Yet something in our life, a power greater than ourselves, valued us even when we did not have the wherewithall to value ourselves.

· 🌿 ·

It's time to give up getting my identity through my problems.

Sleepwalking

One who is pretending to sleep cannot be awakened.

—ANONYMOUS

We addicts really try to look "normal." Yet often we are the only ones fooled.

Our addictions turn us into sleepwalkers. We must first recognize that we are sleepwalking before we can see the need to awaken. One who is pretending to be awake cannot be awakened either.

• ❧ •

Those who love me have often tried to shake me awake, but my pretending made it impossible for them to succeed.

Arrogance

PERSON 1: *One of the things that really gets my goat is that there are so many people starting up at these Twelve-Step meetings, it is taking the focus off of real addicts.*

PERSON 2: *Who are the real addicts?*

PERSON 1: *People who have my addiction.*

—AWS

A rrogance and self-centeredness come in many forms. Why is it that what I have is always "the best," even if it is my addiction? How come we practice our addiction around our addiction?

• ⚘ •

Well, after all, there have to be some areas where we are consistent!

Hanging In

I didn't really think that I was a relationship addict until I heard myself saying that my marriage was terrible but I was hanging in there because there was a point, perhaps two years ago, when my spouse and I were actually able to communicate for a full five minutes. "Who could ask for anything more?"

—ANONYMOUS

It doesn't take much to keep our happy little addictions going.

That's what they mean about the "insanity" of this disease. Addicts are experts at repeating something that doesn't work.

· ❧ ·

I may not get an A for awareness, but I sure get one for the ability to hang in with something that's not working.

Security

A cling-clung relationship may offer a lot of security, but who wants to be married to a roll of flypaper?

—AWS

Security, security. We are willing to sell our souls for the illusion of security. Yet we find that all of our well-chosen fixes—booze, drugs, money, relationships, food, and so forth—don't really give us what we think we need no matter how hard we hold on to them. Our illusion of security is just that, an illusion.

· ❧ ·

When there's no intimacy, it's really important to be glued together.

Sticking with the Shit

A man was sitting in a restaurant over a cup of coffee, obviously very depressed. "What's wrong?" said the waiter. No response. "What's wrong?" "It's my job. I shovel elephant shit in the circus. Tons and tons of elephant shit every day. I can't stand it!" "Why don't you quit?" "What! and leave show business?!!"

—GOLDIE IVENER

We addicts have something in common with the elephant shit shoveler. We complain about the tons of shit we have to wade through, yet we can't imagine just walking away from it.

Where would the excitement be? What would make us feel alive?

• 🌿 •

Anyone ready to turn in their shovel?

Advice—Humility

How many codependents does it take to change a light bulb? Twelve! One puts in the bulb and the other eleven give directions and advice.

—ANONYMOUS

We addicts always know how to do everything right: our way. We are so controlling and stubborn when we are in our disease that we cannot believe that anyone knows how to function as well as we do. After all, look at our lives. Don't they prove our unquestionable competence?

· 🌿 ·

Humility doesn't come easily, and it sure is a relief when it squeezes into our lives.

Helping and Caretaking

*How many recovering codependents does it take
to screw in a light bulb? Twelve! One screws it
in and the other eleven try not to help.*

—Anonymous

Recovery for care-aholics and relationship
addicts is not an easy process. We have to
do more than give up a substance. We have to
give up practicing our disease on everyone and
everything in sight.

The very things that gave us our identities and
gave our lives meaning are up for grabs.

· ❧ ·

It's not that I resent not always helping
out. It's just that others seem so incompe-
tent at times.

Listening—Humility

When I have trouble listening, I usually find out it's because I am doing all the talking.
                                                    —AWS

Humor and humility go hand in hand. Often my budding humility gives me the possibility of seeing the humor in what I am doing. When I am not listening or understanding, it may be because the sound of my own voice sounds infinitely melodious to me. Rested vocal cords and the ability to hear another often go hand in hand.

· 🌿 ·

Just for today, let me know when to shut up!

Spiritual Bankruptcy

I had a lot of husbands, but none of them were mine.

— DIANE C., AS QUOTED IN *Recovering*

The program talks about spiritual bankruptcy. We addicts don't talk about it, we practice it! The process of working the Steps helps us crawl back to integrity. By making amends promptly when we are wrong, little by little we achieve spiritual solvency.

· 🌾 ·

Spiritual bankruptcy takes the meaning out of everything else.

July

Anchoring Our Lives

What little of the ozone that is left—I was in it.

—AWS

When I feel like I'm in outer space, I'm so grateful that I had a rope tied around my leg with an anchor on it. It's called children.

· 🌱 ·

I learn so much from my children. What I sometimes, in my addict's disease, thought were shackles have turned out to be anchors for learning and living.

Facing Fear

Work the Steps and join us. Don't worry about overstepping the truth and becoming a spiritual giant in our times.
—SAM MEIER (SERENITY SAM)

Our favorite fears are usually in the service of our disease. It's a tricky disease and it scrambles to keep its claws in us. The more frightened we are of living, of growing, and of being ourselves, the more tempting it is to use an addiction—old or new—as a security blanket. Go on! Take the risk of becoming a spiritual giant and see what happens!

• 🌿 •

They say, "Faith is fear that has said its prayers."

Going Nuts

If I had a dollar for every time I slipped into my disease, I'd be a wealthy woman. Then again, it hardly seems right to get rich from going nuts.

—AWS

We addicts know how to do "nuts." In fact the nuttiest aspect of going nuts is that it seems normal to us. This abnormal sense of normal may be the norm for the society, but it's still not normal for us. Unfortunately when we have an abnormal norm, being "normal" is a little scary.

· ❧ ·

There's no such thing as a normal addict. That's a relief.

Fireworks

To me it wasn't love unless there were Roman candles going off in the background.

—MARY J.

Not just the Fourth of July but every day of the year, romance addicts look for Roman candles as a "sign." Addicts love excitement and they jazz up their days with crisis.

• 🌿 •

Did you ever notice that too many fireworks destroy the senses?

Having a Disease, Not Being Our Disease

Well, I can rightly say I never met a recovering addict that I didn't like. I didn't give two hoots for his/her disease, though.
—AWS

It is so important to remember that we *have* a disease, we *are not* our disease. We are sick people getting well, not bad people getting good. As our sobriety grows, we can, however, often get a small glimpse of why some of those we love are not too excited about our disease. It's not just "bad taste" on their part, as we had previously thought.

· ✼ ·

I am grateful to experience the growing lack of sync between me and my disease.

"Wet Noodles"

I just discovered the difference between passivity and surrender. I don't think my Higher Power wants to relate to a wet noodle.

—KAREN

I've been in the soup so long I feel like a wet noodle, just lying there, waiting to be devoured, passive, spineless. Somehow the image does not turn one on.

• ❧ •

When I surrender, I have to be *present* to turn it over.

Character Defects

When I think of the range and diversity of my character defects, I feel like a mosquito in a nudist colony. I know what I want to do. I just don't know where to start.

—ANONYMOUS

It's wonderful to have so many opportunities to work on ourselves. It's not just the number of character defects that can keep us busy, it's also the endless facets that each presents.

• ❧ •

I always knew that I was a diamond in the rough.

Truth and Love

The world is too dangerous for anything but truth and too small for anything but love.
—WILLIAM SLOAN COFFIN

When we don't realize the need for truth and love, the world is a pretty scary place. *Truth* and *love* are not just abstract concepts, even if they have been in our lives.

· 🌿 ·

Truth is not dangerous. Truth is not destructive. (Contrary to popular addictive opinion.)

Knowing What's Important

Our biggest fight around getting married was over getting a power lawn mower—and we don't even have a lawn!!
—BILL

I always say, under times of stress a good addict always knows what's important. Of course who has ever seen a bad addict?

· 🌿 ·

When we can't deal with the important, we always focus on the trivial.

Justification

How come I feel that I have to justify my relationship (romance) addiction to a bunch of addicts?
—AWS

As addicts we justify, knowing that no one will believe us anyway. If they do believe us, we lose all respect for them.

· ❧ ·

Probably the only person who really believes an addict is another addict. Recovery is a loss of the need to justify.

Illusions

My image of my childhood is one of asking,
"Are we being Donna Reed yet, Mom?"
—ANONYMOUS

We knew where we were supposed to go. We just didn't know how to get there. At least, we *thought* we knew where we were supposed to go.

• ❧ •

Growing up in a dysfunctional family is growing up looking outside for a clue—any clue—on what to do. Recovery is being able to do without a clue.

Owning the Disease

My Grandpa Willey always said, "The nice thing about a cow is that if you stand close to it, it can't kick you. A horse can kick in any direction, but if you get close to a cow, it can't get you."

—AWS

Addictions are sort of like cows. When we deny them and try to stand back from them, we get some terrible licks. When we cozy up to them, owning them and admitting that we are powerless over them (and keep admitting that and admitting that!), they have trouble "getting in a good one."

• ☙ •

Grandpa's wisdom wasn't only limited to cows.

Self-Improvement

Where can you a find a codependent? In the self-help section of a bookstore. —MIKE FINN

We relationship addicts (or codependents) are never enough. No matter what we do or how well we do it, we are never enough. We are schlepps for self-improvement. If we could just find the right formula, we could make ourselves acceptable.

· ✻ ·

Who are we to improve on God's handiwork?

Perfection

We want to have the absolute perfect recovery and do everything absolutely right (so we can be absolutely happy all the time).
—LINDA ATKINS, AS QUOTED IN *Recovering*

Is it too much to ask that everything be perfect? I am sure that I read somewhere that all these absolutes are our inalienable rights. Or was it the "pursuit" of happiness? If I could get my rights right, maybe I could figure out how to pursue them.

· ❧ ·

I have a right to be sober, happy, and—me.

Inconvenience

I wish someone would invent a convenient *addiction.*

—ANONYMOUS

I'm willing to look at the *convenient* ones. Unfortunately, when I really start looking at them, they all become *inconvenient.* Now I see that they interfere with my life, but they were so easy at first.

Whoever said that being an addict was convenient? But we get so screwed up that recovery starts to look inconvenient to us. I wish there were a convenience store for recovery.

There is, and it's only Twelve Steps away.

"We" Program

I don't know about the DT's anymore, but the CT's (contagious terrors) still get me.
—ANONYMOUS

Some folks may think that we addicts are a little sticky about sticking together. Somehow we'd rather take the risk of catching recovery. One can never be too cautious!

· 🌿 ·

Sobriety requires support, so does addiction. The choice is ours.

Belonging—Families

"Sometimes I feel like a motherless child,"
and a fatherless child, and a sisterless child,
and a brotherless . . . in fact, if there had
been any less of my family, no one would
have been there at all.
                                        —AWS

I must have been adopted. I'm sure I was adopted. Surely I was adopted.

I just don't fit into all this craziness. I've asked my parents and they say no, you're ours. Are they lying? I just don't belong.

· 🌿 ·

When we think we don't belong, that's probably right where we need to be.

My Life

Overheard at a Twelve-Step meeting: "It's not a big deal. It's just my life."
—Trish

Our lives really are a pretty big deal, even if we don't always act like they are. To us they're important.

· 🌿 ·

The sacred can be familiar when we get to know ourselves.

Mixed Up

I'm not confused, I'm just well mixed.
—ROBERT FROST

Some of us specialize in being a tall, exotic drink—well mixed up, without a straw, and all "lickered up."

· 🌿 ·

No matter how you stir it, confusion is being mixed up.

Being Out of Touch

You can't depend on your judgment when your imagination is out of focus.
—MARK TWAIN

O ur addictions put us out of touch with our feelings, our thoughts, our awareness, our imagination, *and* our knowing. No wonder addicts get progressively boring—to themselves and others.

· 🌿 ·

You can't focus your imagination when you can't focus your senses, and judgmentalism puts everything out of focus.

Integrating Our Childhood

Everything else you grow out of, but you never recover from childhood.
—BERYL BAINBRIDGE

Trying to separate from our childhood is like trying to get rid of used flypaper. It not only sticks to us, it has flies on it. And flies are a source of protein.

· 🌿 ·

We never know what will nourish us once we integrate it.

People Pleasing

I don't know the key to success, but the key to failure is trying to please everybody.
—BILL COSBY

How many of us have believed that we were trying to please everyone else when, indeed, we were just trying to get what we wanted! We grew so controlling in our belief that we could please others that no one was happy.

· 🌿 ·

People pleasing is built-in failure.

One Step at a Time

*What's all this fuss about just taking one step
at a time? Did you ever see anyone take two?*
—AWS

The only thing that I know that can success-
fully take more than one step at a time is a
centipede. Have you ever tried walking with both
feet in the air? Impossible, isn't it?

· 🌿 ·

If I take one step at a time, I have to have
one foot on the ground.

Responsibility—Listening

Shut up! Take the cotton out of your ears and put it in your mouth.
— ANONYMOUS

Recovery is not only being responsible for what we put in our bodies; it is being responsible for what we spew out of our mouths. When we start to listen more, we talk less and what we say makes more sense.

When I start to listen, it's amazing what important things others have to say.

Gratitude

People tell me to look for the silver lining when things get bad. With my money addiction, I'd rather have a gold one.

—AWS

When we are in our addiction, it (whatever "it" is) is never enough. We want more. One of the joys of recovery is that we begin to appreciate the little things and know that we have exactly what we need. Surprisingly we may not need as much as we thought we did.

· 🌿 ·

Thanks! Gratitude is not my strong suit—yet!

Being "Natural"

I wanted to be natural. Then I decided maybe I'm just naturally uptight.
—Anonymous

How discouraging! All of this wonderful New Age stuff about just being natural, but what if we are just naturally someone we don't like. "Aye, there's the rub," and a big rub it 'tis.

· 🌿 ·

Frankly I've never seen someone become a person they didn't like when they became themselves, *and* there always is a first time. Anyway this idea gives us something to worry about, and worrying always feels familiar.

Our Garbage

*All of us carry around garbage bags. It's
when they start to leak that we notice.*
—JO LIPPINCOTT

There's nothing worse than a leaky garbage
bag. Garbage is supposed to be contained
and kept in its place.

Yet with our personal garbage bags, we are
fortunate when they start to leak. At least then
we have the opportunity to "notice" our trail,
and we may even begin to clean up some of our
old garbage.

A leaky garbage bag is sort of like being a
grateful alcoholic. The stench gets our attention.

Getting "High"

Recovery, like life, just has too short a honeymoon.
—ANONYMOUS

We addicts can get high on anything—even recovery. Unfortunately recovery highs, like any other highs, don't last, and then we have to return to work our program. We can't stay on our pink cloud forever, and often pretty sunsets are all we need.

· ☙ ·

Highs are short-lived. Serenity is a long-distance runner.

Removing Defects—Step Six

I thought I was doing pretty well with recovery until I got to the step about becoming entirely willing for God to remove my defects. That stopped me short, so I took a six-month vacation from the program just to check it out.

—AWS

Sometimes we go sailing along with the Twelve-Step program and then we have the sudden realization that this program means business and requires a certain dedication. Dedication we have—dedication sometimes *to what* seems kinda foggy.

· ❀ ·

We know how to be dedicated to our disease. Dedication to sobriety seems less clear.

Bargaining—Denial

Being a "little" codependent (addicted) is just like being a little pregnant. It just doesn't compute.
—ANONYMOUS

Sometimes, in our disease, we try to bargain and avoid facing the fact that we are addicted or codependent and that it's time to get on with the process of recovery. We want to believe that we just have a "little addiction." Unfortunately, coming from that perspective, our bargaining power is not that great and our store of resources is not too attractive.

· 🌿 ·

Denial may have some rewards, but I haven't discovered what they are yet.

Fun

I'm having severe fun.

—Bob Brounstein

Remember laughter? Remember humor? Remember just fooling around without *trying* to fool around? Most of us knew how to enjoy life at one time.

Even though most of us delude ourselves into thinking that our addictions will give us a good time and give us what we want, we have come to realize that in addiction there is a certain "joylessness" to our lives in spite of the quick fixes.

· ❧ ·

Lightening up never hurt anybody.

August

Reality

Relationships are always better in the abstract.
                                        —AWS

E very good relationship and romance addict knows that the fantasy of the relationship is better than the relationship. Fantasy is the romance addict's drug.

· ❧ ·

Reality is the stuff that ruins what dreams are made of.

Confusion

*If you haven't all the things you want, be
grateful for all the things you don't have that
you didn't want.*   —ANONYMOUS

Figure and ground get confused in this disease. It's hard to know what's important and
what's not. Also, what's figure to me may be
ground to you. Just try not to get ground up in
figuring out what's figure and what's ground.

· ✺ ·

When I'm grateful for what I have, I don't
need much.

Willingness

Sometimes I have too much willingness. I ooze willingness. I sit there the whole day and try to turn sloth into meditation.

—SAM MEIER (SERENITY SAM)

Being open and willing is great, but if I'm open and I'm oozing willingness, I may become a puddle—I know that place: *Slippery When Wet.* Willingness frequently involves doing something.

Willingness without action is just another form of wiliness.

Illusions—DT's

I do tell you when I first came to AA, something was crawling on me. I spent a long time looking for what it was and never did find out. I'd be sitting in one of those meetings and have one of those spasms, and everybody would think I'd found it.

—Tom O'Sullivan

Sometimes the reason we can't find what we're looking for is because it isn't there. Other times it's because we're not there.

• • •

When my illusions become more real to me than reality, I'm not being realistic about reality.

Humor

We called the dog Addie for addictions. *If we had been working on sexual addictions, we could have called her Adelaide.*
— MAUREEN

D on't tell me addicts don't have a good sense of humor! Unfortunately too often the rest of the world has trouble getting the joke.

· 🌿 ·

When I can laugh at my disease, I know that I'm recovering.

Denial

I've been looking at denial. That's a river in Egypt, isn't it?
— ANONYMOUS

Denial is a form of distancing. Unfortunately what we put at a distance is ourselves.

· ⚘ ·

Denial, dishonesty, distancing, dualism— the four cornerstones of the addictive house of cards.

Memory

Our memories are card indexes—consulted and then put back in disorder by authorities whom we do not control. —CYRIL CONNOLLY

They say that addicts have no memory. If I could just remember what I don't remember, I could know whether it's true or not.

· ❧ ·

If I have no memory, I don't have to worry about forgetting things.

"Iffing"

Yearning is not only a good way to go crazy but also a pretty good place to hide out from hard truth.
—JOY COCKS

If only, what if, as if—the three "realities" of the addict. No wonder everything is so confusing. I wonder if truth could possibly be any more difficult. Truth *can* be stranger than fiction, but never stranger than some of the fiction I concocted on my way to the truth.

· ⚹ ·

My escapes from reality are more than flights of fancy. In fact there's nothing fancy about my flights.

Judgment

When they drank, they had the brains of a chocolate penguin.
—DENNIS

These days there are a lot of decisions being made by chocolate penguins. The problem is they think they're just normal folks. In fact the Chinese have declared a "Year of the Penguin." The problem is, the penguins among us think they're just normal folks. Even in recovery we have to watch out for chocolate-covered decisions.

· 🌱 ·

Perspective and judgment are two of the things we lose in our disease. There are many others.

Clarity

When I'm in my disease, clarity is so confusing.

—AWS

When I'm in my disease, confusion seems confusing, too, but normal. When confusion has become the norm, clarity seems too bright and too stark. We aren't really sure we can bear it. Plus, we don't have to worry about it too often.

· 🌿 ·

If I am beginning to feel comfortable with clarity, I am probably in recovery.

Give Me a Break

The worst place to be is a bellyful of booze and a head full of AA.
—GLEN

Many of us in early recovery see only that our options to behave in our old patterns are melting like ice in the Sahara. The words that often spring to our lips are, "Give me a break!" Fortunately recovery does, indeed, give us a break—a chance to break the habit.

· 🌿 ·

Recovery doesn't mean we have less options, it just means we have less options with which we are familiar.

Control

Self will cannot be overcome by self will.
—ANONYMOUS

I do have to do it myself and I cannot do it *by* myself. When I think that others trying to run my life is my problem, I'm probably looking for trouble in the wrong place.

· ✵ ·

Arrogance and control are blinders to powerlessness, and admitting powerlessness is the beginning of healing power.

Being Crazy

You cannot really get hurt mountain climbing over mole hills.
—Anonymous

It's easier to make the world crazy than to admit our own insanity—and we have the power to make the world unbelievably crazy!

· 🌿 ·

If *I* am the greatest power in the world, the situation's worse than I thought.

Being Understood

When I am sure that God doesn't understand me, I'm probably putting the focus of the confusion in the wrong place.

—AWS

My life has been a search for someone who really understands me. Of course nobody *really* understands me.

I even gave God a chance to understand me and He (She, It) flubbed the opportunity. Consequently I'll just have to do it myself.

· ⚘ ·

Removing my life and will from God is not as easy as I thought.

Focusing on Others

Focusing on others is the drug of choice for the relationship addict.

—AWS

There's no better way to give our power away than to focus our lives on others and what they have done to us.

· ❧ ·

It's hard work, taking everyone else's inventory. Worst of all, they don't even seem grateful.

Arrogance

Plaque on wall:
"Good morning, Joe. This is your Higher
Power speaking. I won't be needing your help
today."
—Anonymous

In our arrogance we often put ourselves at the center of the universe and expect others to have the good sense to orient their lives around us. Arrogance requires stinkin' thinkin' for its continuation.

· ❧ ·

After all, why can't others see that I know what's best for them? Can't they see how well I have done with my life?

Defects

For years I thought if I just got myself fixed up I could fix others. Now what I know is wrong with me is thinking there is something wrong with me (and others). —MARYLOU

It's clear to me what they need to do. I'd think they would be grateful to have such a God-like creature in their life. I know that I know what's good for them, even if they cannot see the wisdom in my words. Surely they can see that a person of my stature and clarity would do wonders for their life.

· 🌿 ·

Yet, if I wait for them to ask for my help, they might never do it—so, a little assertion here, a little assertion there. It couldn't hurt. (Or could it?)

Absence

If you're thinking about committing suicide in the first five years of recovery, you're killing the wrong person.
                                           —ANONYMOUS

What seems like a good idea to someone who isn't there can change completely when we finally arrive.

· 🌿 ·

Killing myself seemed more acceptable than murdering someone else, especially when neither of us was there.

Character Defects

For a sex and love addict, getting into a new relationship is like putting Miracle Grow on all your character defects.
ANONYMOUS

Character defects are like seeds. They are always there waiting to sprout.

· 🌿 ·

With all my bullshit, who needs Miracle Grow.

Revenge

Revenge is one of my techniques to avoid myself.

—AWS

With my arrogance, confusion, stinkin' thinkin,' dishonesty, and anger, I am in an excellent position to get even. In fact, getting even may be my contribution to keeping the universe in balance—and no one has a better sense of balance than I do.

• • •

When I am focused upon getting even with others, I have left myself and am out of balance with me.

Self-Abuse

It's hard for a self-abuser to get too much of a bad thing.
—AWS

Self-abuse is the cornerstone of addiction. An improper cornerstone can support a shaky life.

· 🌿 ·

When I am self-abusing, at least I'm getting attention.

Absence

Suddenly is what happens when I am not paying attention.

—Anonymous

Accidents, suddenly, surprises, crisis . . . exciting, aren't they? Too bad we're not there to get the real thrill.

• • •

When I'm not there, I'm not anywhere.

Survival

ADDICT: *I can't see what's so important about Step Twelve.*

SPONSOR: *Don't worry, you have eleven steps to go before that need concern you.*

—ANONYMOUS

We have survived, haven't we? That must prove something. It does. It proves we don't know much about *living*.

· ❧ ·

When we get to a place where we believe that survival is all there is, it's time to hope that there is someone else around who needs to do some Twelve-Step work and they find us.

Losing Ourselves

When they say, "Will the real Elaine please stand up?" I'm afraid no one will.

—ELAINE

There's something we seem to have lost track of years ago—ourselves: feeling selves, thinking selves, spiritual selves, trusted selves, the selves of self.

· ❧ ·

What some folks think of as "gone" is usually just well hidden.

Wimpdom

We have never had a Chicken Shit Anonymous meeting. Everyone is afraid to come.

—JOHN

There are so many roads to wimpdom: nice-ness, dishonesty, people pleasing, and fear. And the superhighway leading to oblivion is paved with little pieces of discarded selves held together by silence and dishonesty.

· 🌿 ·

Sometimes when we get scared to "put ourselves out there," it is a relief to know that we have a *someone* to show and tell.

Childhood

The thing that impresses me the most about America is the way parents obey their children.
—EDWARD, DUKE OF WINDSOR

We addicts never felt that anyone was in charge or that we had a childhood. If parents aren't parenting, how can children risk childrening?

I am the integration of all my experiences. The issue is not so much what those experiences were. The issue is that I own them.

· 🌿 ·

If poor parenting were fatal, we would not have to worry about population problems. We are more than what our parents created.

Smiling

Wrinkles should merely indicate where smiles have been.
—MARK TWAIN

Forgetting how to smile is part of an addict's memory loss.

· ❧ ·

Luckily smiling is an activity our face can still remember.

Bingeing

Life itself is the proper binge.

—JULIA CHILD

We addicts are bingers. We will binge on anything that limits living. After a while the vehicle for the binge loses its importance and the binge takes on a death of its own.

· 🌿 ·

If you must binge, do it on living fully.

Intimacy

There are men I could spend eternity with,
but not in this life.   —KATHLEEN NORRIS

Addictions are hard on relationships. We want them, and we don't quite know how to do them. We are good at taking hostages, we just don't know how to have partners.

Maybe I can't make intimacy happen, and I *do* hope I have it happen in this lifetime. I'd hate to miss it, and with recovery I pray that I'll recognize it when it happens.

· ⚘ ·

Recovery not only means recovering ourselves, it also means recovering the possibility of being intimate.

Being Unconscious

Being unconscious is great for sleeping, but it's not too effective for living.
—AWS

Being in my disease was like going through life with a sleep mask on. Somehow I came to believe that if I just didn't see or feel what was going on in my life, it wasn't happening.

• ❧ •

When I am conscious in my living, I may feel pain, but I also have the possibility of feeling joy, happiness, serenity, and even love.

Progress, Not Perfection

I never did deny that I had a problem. I just thought it was important not to emphasize the negative.

—AWS

Good one! Aren't addicts slick? I just love it. We will find ingenious ways of protecting our supply.

One of our favorites is to try only to let go of certain aspects of our disease while maintaining our image to ourselves and others. We would rather ignore the rigors of recovery. Luckily we don't have to do it all at once. That's why there are Twelve Steps.

· ❧ ·

Crawl when you can't walk. Just keep moving. Remember, it's progress, not perfection.

September

·❦·

Giving Ourselves Away

I knew a woman once who lived in a household consisting of herself, her husband, and their three sons. So that the men in the house would not be inconvenienced, she always put the toilet seat up after she went to the bathroom.

—AWS

Sometimes we don't even notice when we are giving little pieces of ourselves away. Over time, suddenly there is seemingly nothing left. Trying to be invisible so as not to annoy is one of the traits of the codependent.

• 🌿 •

Being codependent is like grease spots on a silk blouse. They can fade but they never completely go away.

Reality

An alcoholic by himself is bad company.
—ERNIE LARSEN

Before we started our recovery, our reality testing wasn't bad—it was nonexistent.

• ❧ •

In recovery I have learned that the one good thing about reality is that it is real.

Confused Thinking

*They think children are cement for a
crumbling marriage. They're not, they're
hand grenades.*
—CHRIS

Anytime we look for an external solution for an internal problem, things blow up. Any "fix" will do when we refuse to recognize the real problem.

• ☙ •

How can I know the right answers when I don't know the right questions?

Stinkin' Thinkin'

*When I am in my disease, I am very logical
and rational. I just don't make any sense.*
—AWS

My most logical, rational moments may be the ones when I am farthest from the truth—mine and others'. I find that I often resort to the excessiveness of rational, logical thinking when I feel threatened or when I want to be in control. Both states, hopefully, will signal that I am in my disease and need to get back to my program and my sobriety.

· ✿ ·

Not making any sense isn't just reserved for people we call crazy.

We Are Not Our Disease

*You name it, I've been there. I thought my
name was "Get in the car, punk."*
—SAM MEIER (SERENITY SAM)

I dentities get kinda squirrely with this disease.
Actually, at one point I thought I was one and
I started gathering nuts around me. Of course, I
fit right in.

· 🌿 ·

We *have* a disease, we *are not* our disease.

Isolation

When I was living in my disease, I thought I was the only one who felt this way. It's amazing how many people have come down with it since I started to recover.

—AWS

F ear and isolation are big components of this disease. The sicker we get, the more we isolate. It's not that others are not there for us; we just can't see them.

• 🌿 •

Addiction doesn't just alter my mood and brain; it also seems to make me progressively nearsighted.

Dropping Out

*One thing positive was, after I quit bathing,
you never had trouble finding a seat at AA;
there was always one on each side of me and
one in front and one in back.*
— Tom O'Sullivan

Once we get seriously into our addictions,
we are better able to tell what's really important and we let go of the little unimportant
things, such as bathing, eating, paying bills. In
recovery we may need to relearn some basic skills.
I know one fellow who had a laundry sponsor.

• ❧ •

When I dropped out on myself, people
stopped dropping in on me.

Clarity

If I don't know whether I'm clear or not, I'm probably not.
—CONSTANCE

I can keep so busy trying to figure things out that I never have to take the risk of doing them.

· ❧ ·

Clarity is not something we figure out.

Shame

*The more shame I feel, the more secure I feel.
I use it for the mortar for the bricks to build
my wall.*

—AWS

When shame becomes an old, comfortable friend, one would think that's a clue that something is wrong. Shame cults can protect the disease like any other addictive behavior.

· ⚘ ·

Nurturing my shame is like sleeping with a pet cobra. It certainly keeps others out of my life, but I'd better not turn my back on it.

Dishonesty

It was my dishonesty about my dishonesty that finally tripped me up.

—AWS

Just when I thought I had all my bases covered, I discovered I wasn't playing baseball.

· ⚘ ·

Life is all in the way you pitch it. We throw most of the curveballs ourselves.

Today

God made the world round so we would never be able to see too far down the road.
—Isak Dinesen

We addicts always want to have road maps, know where we're going before we start, and see the future spread out before us. What better way not to have to live today.

• ❧ •

If I miss today, tomorrow doesn't have a very good base to build upon.

Owning Our Lives

Hindsight is an exact science.
—GUY BELLAMY

Hindsight may be an exact science, but not when it is drugged with addiction! It is only as we get clear that we can *own* our life for what it was, what it is, and whatever it will be.

· 🌱 ·

As I clear my brain and being, I can accept my life—I think!

Overkill

I'm the kind of person who tends to use a bazooka to kill a fly.
—DIANE

Overkill is a characteristic of the disease. At least it adds a little excitement, but sometimes everyone disappears in the excitement. When I raise a bazooka to kill a fly, I have to spend a lot of time digging through the rubble.

· ✣ ·

Sometimes I had to go to extraordinary means to know I was still alive.

Balance

What does it mean to be a well-balanced addict? One has a nice, creative spread of addictions.

—ANONYMOUS

We addicts are very creative—we seek balance in everything. Why settle for one addiction when we can develop a creative balance of substance and process addictions? No harm in having it all. We not only can drink and smoke, we can overwork, overspend, and generally abuse ourselves. Addicts are creative in ways to practice addiction.

· ✿ ·

When I feel off-balance in my disease, I may be in balance.

The "Soaps"

I learned relationships in the "soaps."
—Anonymous

Soap operas always seemed to be one of the more concrete examples of reality in my life. They never had a dull moment, created a crisis a minute, and developed such complex plots—and everybody was *involved*.

· ⚘ ·

It's much better to *watch* a soap opera than to *live* one.

Distortions

*All of us have shit detectors somewhere. I used
to think mine was in my gonads.*
—GLEN

Funny how our knowledge of anatomy becomes confused. If we want to stay in our disease, our information should always be in the service of the disease. One does wonder sometimes where we addicts process our information.

· 🌿 ·

As a friend of mine said, "I always knew that I had a committee in my head. Only recently did I realize that they're all addicts."

Life Scripts

When the scripts for life were passed out, I was still in the dressing room.

—ANONYMOUS

Somehow we addicts always feel like we are missing something. Everyone else seems to have more information than we do. Everyone seems to know something we don't. If we just had a script, we would certainly *try* to get it right.

· 🌿 ·

We addicts *do* have a life script. Unfortunately when we try to write it, the *playwright* is an addict.

Insight

Insight is the booby prize of life (if you don't act on it).

—DEAN C., AS QUOTED IN *Recovering*

Not using our insights is like saying, "I'm in my disease," and going ahead and staying in it. Or like attending meetings and not working a program. Or like saying, "I'm recovered."

• ❧ •

We addicts have won so many booby prizes, it seems strange that we would need to compete for one more. Actually we don't *need* to.

Hitting Bottom

I was hit by so many bottoms that I felt like a public toilet.
— DEAN C., AS QUOTED IN *Recovering*

And you know what goes down a public toilet! Do we really want to become familiar with so many bottoms? There are other ways of making contact.

• ✣ •

We always say, "From a bottom there's only one direction—up."

Arrogance

*Twenty-five years friends and I'm going to
work her program for her. That's friendship,
isn't it?*
—ANONYMOUS

After all this time I surely know more about
her than she knows about herself. Isn't
friendship when we worry about, take care of,
and know what's best for? That's what I learned
in my family.

· 🌿 ·

Who said families are the best teachers
about friendships?

Shame

Shame is something I know on a cellular level.
                                              —GAIL

The scientists have not located a "shame gene" yet, but if we have one, it's probably in hiding.

· ❧ ·

Shame goes pretty deep, but it's probably more learned than earned.

Bingeing

The way I binge with my addiction reminds me of the way I try to talk with my husband when he is watching the football games. I sit there holding everything in and then I blurt out everything during the commercials.

—CARLA

Is it any wonder that we often feel unheard? We store and puke, store and puke, and store and puke, and then we wonder why others aren't thrilled to be the recipient of our flow of words.

· 🌿 ·

Bingeing is bingeing, whether it is done with food, booze, or words.

Spiritual Awakening

A dead atheist is someone who's all dressed up with no place to go.
—JAMES DAFFECY

Before we have a spiritual awakening, we keep running, but it is as if one foot is nailed to the floor. We have no place to go with ourselves.

· 🌿 ·

Perhaps our Higher Power is the one with the crowbar who can pry us loose when we are stuck. I'm glad someone has a tool!

Relationship Addiction

All her life she's loved two kinds of men: the ones she still desired after she knew they were wrong for her, and the ones she remained tied to long after she lost all desire.

—ALIX KATES SHULMAN

A ddictive relationships! What a wonderful way to escape from intimacy! Who needs 'em? Addicts—that's who!

· 🌿 ·

Relationship addiction seems so normal. Actually, it is—but that doesn't mean we have to continue in it.

Dimensional Life

We had seen the light at the end of the tunnel, and it was out.
—JOHN C. CLANCY

Now you see it, now you don't. Recovering isn't linear. For recovery to be linear, we would have to be two-dimensional. Addictions are multidimensional diseases; they affect every aspect of our lives.

• 🌿 •

Now's our chance to recover in multi-dimensions.

Caretaking

*It seems as if I have spent all my life helping
other people, and now I'm expected to help
other people with their recovery. Of course, they
need it a lot worse than I do.*

—ANONYMOUS

There's just no end to caretaking, is there?
Unfortunately caretakers tend to be a little
farsighted. They can't see up close—themselves,
for example.

· 🌿 ·

When I start taking a good, hard look at
myself, I find that I have less time to scrutinize others.

Showing Up for Life

When I answered that all were present and accounted for, I was speaking for someone else. I never made it that day. —ANONYMOUS

S howing up for life is not something we are accustomed to doing on a regular basis. In fact, our addictions often help us avoid that necessity.

In recovery we find that we are capable of being present to life, and it is shocking, what fun that can be.

· 🌿 ·

Gone today, gone tomorrow has changed to here today, here tomorrow.

Self

*The problem with all these self-help books is
that there has to be a self there to help.*

—ANONYMOUS

S elfhood and self-centeredness are different
beasts. Selfhood often gets drowned by self-
centeredness during the throes of our disease,
and we come to believe that we no longer *have*
a self.

Fortunately, our selfhood never goes away. It
just gets buried under layers of character defects.

As we recover and work through our layers of
disease, we discover that there is someone there,
someone worth loving.

· ❧ ·

Formulae will never create a self. God created a self. I have only to uncover it.

Walking the Walk

HE: *How many times have I told you that you have to do it yourself?*

SHE: *I reckon the same number of times you have told me* how *I should do it.*

—AWS

Sometimes we learn the language of recovery and the true meaning of what we are saying does not quite "sink into our innards." We are not above using the insights of recovery to "protect our supply." Happily we get what we are ready to handle—no more, no less. It is often our defensiveness that turns a potential giggle into a war.

· 🌿 ·

Using addiction to protect my addiction is still addiction.

Crisis

For an addict, something's wrong when nothing is.

—AWS

We like crisis. We are familiar with crisis. Most of us grew up in households where we were living with a centipede and we were always waiting for the other shoe to fall. Crisis we understand, calm makes us nervous.

• ❧ •

Show me a crisis and I'll show you a happy addict.

October

·❧·

Fooling People

*I never could figure out what was so attractive
about zombiehood. Zombies can't think, they
drool slightly, they have no life of their own,
and they watch a lot of television. I get
it!—they can pass for normal!*

—AWS

As good old Abe said, "You can fool some of
the people some of the time, but you can't
fool all of the people all of the time." Or you can
fool yourself most of the time.

· ✵ ·

Only a fool tries to fool people.

Pain—Gratitude

The pain gives you willingness, your Higher Power gives you recovery.
                    —DEAN C., AS QUOTED IN *Recovering*

It is surprising there hasn't been a significant body of research done on the pain threshold of addicts—and we don't even have kryptonite.

So we identify pain with recovery. Yet we are anesthetized against the pain of our addictions. My pain is mine, my Higher Power helps me use it to change.

· ꕤ ·

When I am grateful for my pain, I know I'm in recovery!

Stinkin' Thinkin'

*Drinking and thinking is worse than
drinking and driving.*
—LANGFORD WILSON

Unfortunately drinking and thinking is even more common than drinking and driving. Drinking and driving is lethal for a few; drinking and thinking can be lethal for us all. Did you ever listen to a nonrecovering addict try to explain why he or she was right? Here we have logic that makes no sense.

• 🌿 •

When my thinking is confused, I am confused about my thinking.

Con

Our cons are frequently so good that we are the only ones fooled.

—AWS

Before I started recovery, I believed my con. I was certain that others could not see through me and that I really had them fooled. As they say, there's no fool like an old fool, and sometimes I was older than I realized.

Facing my con would not have been my choice of a daily exercise routine. Yet anticipating its slipperiness has truly kept me on my toes.

· ❧ ·

Maybe today I will have the opportunity of saying, "Where's the con?"

The Beauty of Tragedy

I always did think that there was something beautiful *about having a drink or two or three and sitting there with tears streaming down my face just* being sad.
—TOM O'SULLIVAN

How wonderful to have chemically induced feelings. How romantic! How beautifully tragic! How wonderfully sad! How like an addict!

· 🌿 ·

My true feelings are there—inside me, no big deal. Addiction-induced feelings are always more like a dam bursting than like dealing with myself.

Passivity

MO: *What happened to the Passivity Anonymous meeting?*

JOE: *No one called it!*

—ANONYMOUS

What every good Recovery Passivity Anonymous group needs is some good codependent to organize it. I'll do it!

• ❧ •

Remember when someone who was passive looked good because they seemed so controllable? I'm glad that phase of the disease is over.

Higher Power

I'll bet you when you get down on them rusty knees and get to worrying God, He goes in his privy house and slams the door. That's what he thinks about you *and* your *prayers.*
—ZORA NEALE HURSTON

We've been so out of contact with our Higher Power that we are afraid that Power may be like a sensitive parent and slam the door in our face. Making contact is up to us.

· ❧ ·

We'll never know if God's there if we don't try to open our closed doors.

Assumptions

Assumption is the mother of screwup.
—ANGELO DENGHIA

When we act on assumptions, we act out of ignorance and stupidity. Unfortunately in our circles this has been acceptable behavior.

· ❧ ·

Assumptions are like boomerangs. We can innocently toss them out, but they usually return to us just when we least expect it and help us grow knots on our head.

Trusting a Power Greater than Ourselves

An atheist is a man [sic] who has no invisible means of support.
—FULTON J. SHEEN

An addict is a person who has no visible means of support. When we think we have to, and can, do everything by ourselves, we have no visible *or* invisible means of support.

· ❧ ·

Thank goodness that our power greater than ourselves is cunning, baffling, powerful, and patient.

Switching Addictions

When I'm not in the addiction I love, I love the addiction I'm in.
—CHRIS

Addiction switching seems to be more common than partner switching was in the 1960s. Maybe it has been for some time. If we don't recognize that our underlying addictive process can take many forms, we may miss the creative aspects of this disease. *Cunning, baffling, powerful,* and *patient* are not just words, you know.

· ❧ ·

It's so good to have choices.

Starting Recovery

*My life has been like an airplane flying
around on instruments. It's time to land that
thing in a Twelve-Step meeting.*   —Dan

I was beginning to think I was in *The Twilight
Zone.* Maybe I was. Now that I know that I
have the option of landing in a Twelve-Step meeting, I can sigh with relief to know that there are
some landing pads somewhere.

· ❧ ·

When I was flying around in my addictions, I didn't realize that I had cut off all
communications with myself *and* with the
tower. No wonder it was so hard to land
anywhere but bottom.

Attitudes

I look at the world through shit-colored glasses.
—TERRET

· 🌿 ·

When we look at the world through shit-colored glasses, it is no wonder it looks so unpleasant. There are some steps we can take to get a new prescription and new lenses—even glass cleaner. Recovery steps, for example.

· 🌿 ·

Recovery is like getting a new prescription for life. Our Higher Power writes it, but it's up to us to fill it and choose the frames.

Impression Management

I wear a peacock suit, but underneath there's a turkey.
—Kim

Impression management is tricky. We aren't always what we seem. Usually when we try to impress others, we don't really know who *we* are.

· ✻ ·

When we are trying to be peacocks, we should probably check and see how many peahens there are around who might be interested. One thing is for sure, there are plenty of turkeys.

Playing Out Our Addictions

I feel like I go through the same sets of feelings over and over. I don't even know why I need different people.
—MARK

Maybe we should give our cast an opportunity to audition. Of course most of them have probably tried out for this play before, too. We may have a new stage setting, and often the roles and the lines sound unbelievably familiar.

· 🌿 ·

When we in desperation ask ourselves how long we have to repeat these painful patterns, the answer comes quickly: We'll do it until it hurts too much.

Ego

I feel kinda like I did when I first started Alcoholics Anonymous. My ego is really tied up in being an "old-timer."
—Susan

One thing about this addiction: Unlike other things in our lives, we can always depend upon it to be there, no matter what form it takes.

· ❧ ·

If there's one thing on which I can depend, it's my ego.

Confusion

In addictive systems we spend most of our time trying to figure out what is going on, when in reality, nothing is.

—AWS

Confusion has become so "normal" to us addicts that we cannot even imagine nonconfusion. Clarity has become associated with gazing through a cold beer. Simplicity, sobriety, and centeredness are not only dimly remembered experiences, they are almost frightening. We fear that we would be totally unproductive if we didn't have a constant "buzz" going.

· ༀ ·

Maybe it's time to recycle the teaching of our childhood: Stop, look, and listen!

Denial

I'm still crazy as hell, but if I don't drink or use, nobody will notice.
—DEAN C., AS QUOTED IN *Recovering*

Those things we expose to the Rockies are usually seen by more than we realize. How arrogant of us to believe that others do not see how crazy we are in our disease. The self-con is the most frequently used con, and it usually has a one-person effectiveness.

· 🌿 ·

The ostrich never thought anyone could see his bottom, either.

Perceptions

"Crazy" is in the eye of the beholder.

—AWS

What you see is what you get. How about contacts?

· 🌿 ·

It's amazing how much saner others seem since I have been doing my recovery work.

Illusion

Your whole life just looks great until you look at it.
                                              —DAVID

Funny how illusion works. You don't know it's an illusion if you don't know reality. And since we are taught that illusion is reality and reality is illusion, it's no wonder we are deluded about illusion.

· 🌿 ·

When I give up my illusions, what's left? Reality.

Living Foolishly

I was earning fifty dollars a week. I spent a third of that on booze and another third on women—the rest I just spent foolishly.

—ANONYMOUS

Sometimes we get confused about what is foolish and what isn't. In our disease our perspective does get a little distorted, doesn't it? Luckily recovery includes a change of perception.

· 🌿 ·

In recovery what's foolish changes. For example, ninety meetings in ninety days seems quite sane.

Money

PERSON 1: *I'm trying to call a Debtors Anonymous meeting.*

PERSON 2: *How much does it cost?*

—VICKI

Maybe the best things in life are free, but it sure has cost a lot to get this much in debt.

· ❧ ·

Nobody ever told me that money was a liquid asset. It runs right through my fingers.

Recovery Process

*Even when you're on the right track, you'll
get run over if you just sit there.*
—WILL ROGERS

I thought there would be some point where I
was just "fixed" and could relax. I keep forgetting that life is a process and I am a process
and we just go on and on. Of course I *try* to
forget that addictions are a process, too!

· ❧ ·

The recovering person who just wants to
rest on her or his laurels is sitting on very
thin ice in very hot soup.

Explanations

We must believe in luck, for how else can we explain the success of those we don't like?
—JEAN COCTEAU

How human it is not to like some people! How diseased it is to believe that our Higher Power doesn't like those people either! How fortunate that our Higher Power is not under our control.

· 🌿 ·

When I need to explain another's success, I'd better take a long, hard look at myself.

Decisions

Now I know what hell is. Hell is perfect ambivalence.
—ALIX KATES SHULMAN

There is a direct correlation between the progression of our disease and our inability to make decisions.

· 🌿 ·

There is nothing funnier than trying to watch the perfect controller make the perfect decision.

Living Extravagantly

The cost of living is going up and the chance of living is going down.
—FLIP WILSON

For the recovering addict, the chances for living get greater and greater with each day of sobriety. It costs less to live sober.

Of course after we have squandered our lives on our addictions, we may have to start sobriety on a budget.

· ❧ ·

Even sobriety on a budget is living life extravagantly.

Letting Go

Why can't I do things my *way? Let's face it.*
Nothing else even compares.
—AWS

How difficult it is for us to give up doing it
"our" way! We can't imagine that anyone
or anything in the universe can direct our lives
better than we can.

Fortunately, as we begin to recover, we start to
realize that we are not alone. We have support on
many different levels, both seen and unseen.

• ❧ •

I thought I was in the driver's seat, but I
wasn't even in the car.

Deadness—Living

I don't want to be brain dead. I want to be life present.
—BETTY W.

If someone asked us if we wanted to be brain dead, most of us would say no. Yet, when we are active in our addictions, we are choosing to become progressively deader in every sphere of our being.

· 🌿 ·

Addiction doesn't just alter my brain and my mood. I also seem to be getting progressively nearsighted.

Fixes

My spouse (partner) often says, "Let's make up and go to bed." That's the damnedest thing. Why would I want to make love with someone I don't like at the moment?

—ANONYMOUS

Fixes, fixes, fixes. The temptation for us addicts is always to go for the quick fix. It may be a drink fix, a sex fix, a money fix, or a relationship fix, and we want it *now*! None of this waiting around for the process to run its course while we do the necessary footwork. We "smart" ones know how to get it (whatever "it" is!) quicker.

· 🌿 ·

Relax. Take it easy. No good addict has to worry about a favorite addiction disappearing overnight.

Short Prayers

Tonight I learned the short version of the
Serenity Prayer: Fuck it.

—JUDY

O ne of my friends said that she always used to be embarrassed by her husband's foul language. Then someone told her that the short form of the Serenity Prayer is "fuck it." Now when he uses this language, she just tells herself that he is praying and it doesn't bother her at all.

· 🌿 ·

A slight shift in perception can make a major shift in relationships.

Trying

Just show me someone who is fully recovered and how they act and I'll do it.
—WENDY

We addicts know "as if." We have spent years trying to act as if we were normal. We are great cons and we are great emulators. We try to figure out what normal is and then we try to do it.

When we discover recovery, we do what we know best: Just tell us how it's done and we'll try to do it (we'll resent it, but we'll try). Just show us someone with a strong program and we'll try to work their program—not ours!

· 🌿 ·

God knows I try. My friends know. I'm trying!

"We" Program

If you don't have a group and a sponsor in recovery, it's kind of like putting Dracula in charge of a blood bank.
—ERNIE LARSEN

Of course going to meetings is kinda like putting the blood bank in charge of Dracula. I wonder why they didn't think of that!

· ❧ ·

We addicts are "minimalists." We always try to see what is the least we can do to get by. Unfortunately the returns are proportionate to our investments.

November

⬩ ❧ ⬩

Feelings—Perfectionism

Sometimes I hear people say that if I were working a good program, I wouldn't have these feelings come up. I didn't know that the program was a form of feeling vaccination. Kinda sounds like what I was trying to do with my addiction.

—AWS

This perfectionism stuff sure is tricky. If I could just figure out how I'm supposed to do it, I'll try. Yet, it seems that the Twelve-Step program is just accepting ourselves the way we are.

· ✿ ·

Trying is dying, they say.

Effects of the Disease

I got into a Mustang that the bank was looking to repossess, but they couldn't recognize it because it looked like an accordion.
—David Oronofsky

Everything around us takes a beating when we're in our disease. Some of it shows physically: our bones, our families, our possessions, our bodies, ourselves.

· 🌿 ·

Addictions are multidimensional diseases; they affect every facet of our lives.

Judgmentalism

People who judge other people for not doing what they say they are doing are usually not doing what *they* say they are doing.

—AWS

F unny how I always see in others what I least want to look at in myself. Of course, if I keep focusing on what *they* are doing wrong, I don't have to look at me.

· ✿ ·

Judgmentalism is part of the addictive diseases. When I am judgmental, I am in my disease.

Enhancing the Trivial

Duty largely consists of pretending that the trivial is critical.
—JOHN FOWLES

We addicts are good at pretending the trivial is critical. We codependents, relationship addicts, and workaholics in our righteousness have the ability to make even the most trivial important. No one ever said that we don't have skills. Sometimes we just wonder what planet they were developed for.

• ❧ •

When we focus on the trivial, we don't have to deal with the important.

Perfectionism

One day when I was feeling angry and depressed, someone said to me that I must not be working a good program. I spent the rest of the day trying to figure out what program, 'cause I sure knew they couldn't be talking about the Twelve-Step program.

—AWS

Perfectionism is so sneaky. Somewhere, somehow, there's just got to be a right way to do it. When we figure out the right way, we can ascend—or at least be better than "those others."

. ※ .

Addicts will try to turn anything into a perfectionism task, even working the Twelve-Step program.

Guilt

Guilt: the gift that keeps on giving.
                                                                —ERMA BOMBECK

If guilt is the gift that keeps on giving, why have some of us tried to convince everyone that we didn't get anything from our families and the Church! Come on, fess up, there are some lifetime gifts we have received. Show appreciation. Shame on you.

· 🌿 ·

When all else fails, I still have my guilt to fall back on.

Owning Our Lives

I am a chronic, compulsive, automatic exaggerator.

—NANCY

When we admit who we are (at the moment), we have the opportunity to change. If we don't admit who we are, we stay stuck.

· 🌿 ·

One thing that is hard to exaggerate is recovery.

Fixes

I'm working so hard on my time management that I don't have time to get anything done.
—ANONYMOUS

The problem with fixes is that they keep us busy while not addressing the problem. Fixes are one good way to protect our supply while carefully looking good. When we don't confront the disease of addiction, we can do lots of good things *and* most of them subtly protect our supply.

· ⚘ ·

Fixes come in many shapes and sizes. The better they look on the outside, the better we like them—especially if they look like recovery and aren't.

Letting Go

*You say "living in process" is like flying by
the seat of your pants—but you have to be in
them.*
　　　　　　　　　　　　　　　—LAURA

To fly by the seat of your pants, you have to
be *in* them. It's better if they're *your* pants.
They have to have a place on them for the celestial sky hook to catch on to, and you have to let
go of that pillar of perfection you have your arms
wrapped around. Is that all? For the time being.

· ❧ ·

If I dare to live my process, I develop an
intimate relationship with the celestial sky
hook.

Living in the Now

What happens when the good codependent keeps one foot in yesterday and one foot in tomorrow?

He/she shits all over today!

—GERRI DEHAVEN

In recovery circles we often hear that analysis is paralysis. Clinging to our past and focusing on our future paralyzes us. If we want to be present, we have to put our feet together and take a stand.

If I take care of today, tomorrow will take care of itself.

My uncle used to say, "Today is the tomorrow you thought about yesterday," and he was an alcoholic.

Self-deception

When you drink in a closet with a light off, nobody knows.

—KIM

When was it we started to believe that when we are all alone, nobody is there?

• ❧ •

When others are not around, it's up to us to make sure someone's there.

Binges

I do a relationship binge just like I did alcohol binges. Every three months I "go off."

—SUSAN

There is really not much difference between alcohol addiction and relationship addiction. The focus may shift, but the patterns are the same. Switching addictions is like changing shirts that haven't been laundered.

· 🌿 ·

One of the reasons we stay in ruts is because they run deep. We need *some* familiar things in our life, don't we?

Change

Well, any change in some lives would be lifesaving, even spare change.
—DEAN C., AS QUOTED IN *Recovering*

Can we afford to change? Can we afford not to? Brother, can you spare a dime? Brother, can I afford to change? Recovery is cheap compared with the disease.

· ❧ ·

I just need to learn to put my money where my mouth is. There is no possibility of payoff unless I start.

Unknowns

This issue is just one more unknown that I know about.
—ANONYMOUS

Hmmmm—makes sense, doesn't it. When we know the unknown, it becomes known unless it's still unknown. Then we have to find out about it.

Our addictions thrive on unknowns. In fact the purpose of addictions is progressively to make more of ourselves and our lives unknown to us. As we begin recovering, we begin to know about our unknowns.

· ❧ ·

Unknowns aren't so bad—when we know about them!!

Remote Controls

You know you are a relationship addict when you can't commit suicide because someone would be angry with you. —CAROL

Relationship addicts are like people with huge rotating satellite dishes, tuning in to the signals of everyone around them. There's no internal control switch. If we look "out there" for our answers, no one is running the show "in here."

· ⚥ ·

Relationship addicts work on remote control. When someone gets remote, they hand the control right over.

Taking the Steps

The elevator to recovery is out of order. You'll just have to use the Steps.
—RONDA GATES

How lucky for us that there is no quick cure for addiction. Otherwise we would not have the time to learn what we need to learn.

· ❧ ·

No express elevators for us and no freight elevators, either. The weight of our freight just can't get through the gate. It's only Twelve Steps, one at a time.

Punishment

Codependents see recovery as a punishment for not having done it right.

—Anonymous

Strange how distorted our thinking becomes that we come to see living fully as a punishment. If we had done it right the first time, we wouldn't have to redo it. Yet our disease has opened doors that we would never have seen without it.

· 🌿 ·

When we worry about getting it right, we forget that we are doing it. Hit me again!

Doing It Ourselves

If you let other people do it for you, they will do it to you.
—ROBERT ANTHONY

R ecovery! We have to do it ourselves. We do not have to do it alone.

• 🌿 •

Whoever heard of someone doing your recovery for you? A good codependent. That's who!

Relationship Insanity

An appeaser is one who feeds a crocodile,
hoping it will eat him last.
                              —WINSTON CHURCHILL

Relationship addicts know about appeasement. We believe that if we can just keep
others happy, they won't go away and we will be
secure and safe. Strange how a good appeasement
can convert a lamb into a crocodile.

· 🌿 ·

Insanity is doing the same thing over and
over even when it never worked in the first
place.

Fixes

*There, across the room, was my cosmic mate,
my partner for the "Some Enchanted Evening"
Syndrome. Suddenly I felt alive and happy.
My fix was there—for a second, that is.*

—AWS

Cosmic mates are about as scary as "the perfect drunk." When we go for the fix, we don't get fixed. Regardless of what our addiction is, that quick fix is so tempting that it's hard to let go of the possibility.

• ❧ •

Why is it, all too often, that "Some Enchanted Evening" is followed by "The Morning After."

Arrogance and Competition

Few things are harder to put up with than the annoyance of a good example.

—MARK TWAIN

Sometimes we get competitive, even in recovery. We come to believe that our disease is the "best" form of addiction and we are the only "real ones who suffer." As we start recovery, we want to have the "best recovery program around." Slowly we learn that recovery and competition have nothing in common.

· 🌿 ·

There's nothing funnier than a holier-than-thou recovering addict—unless it's a holier-than-thou nonrecovering addict.

Confused Thinking

What's on your mind, if you'll allow the overstatement?
—FRED ALLEN

Mind? Mind? What mind? I find it hard to think about what I'm thinking about. Especially when I can't remember what it was I was thinking. Surely this will get better.

· ✿ ·

Isn't there some Eastern religion where mindlessness is a status symbol?

Regrets

Look to the future—your eyes are in the front of your head.
                                                    —ANONYMOUS

Regrets and looking back are excellent techniques for keeping us stuck. Perhaps, if we notice the construction of our anatomy, we will perceive that we have eyes in the front of our head for a reason.

· ❧ ·

Some of us would like eyes in the front of our head, some of us would like eyes in the back, and some of us would prefer a head that rotates like a swizzle stick. Me, I'd just like a clear head, regardless of the direction it points.

Being Specific

Some folks are saying that we can look at Step Three as: I came . . . I came to . . . I came to believe. Good heavens, that's a year's work right there.

—AWS

We addicts like global. Global is better. There is more room to hide than in specifics. Global is amorphous, slippery, unclear, confused. Sound familiar?

If we have to pay attention to the specifics, we run the risk of breaking through our denial system. Yikes!

• 🌿 •

Global, global, global—we're beginning to sound like a Thanksgiving Turkey. You know what happens to turkeys!

Cons

My disease does a marvelous imitation of clarity.
—NANCY E. S.

Our "clarity cons" are some of our best productions. Show us how clear looks and we'll do it (at least we'll sure do a good job of looking like we're doing it!).

Sometimes one does just have to stop in awe of this disease. It really is cunning, baffling, powerful, and patient. To be sure, we haven't chosen (or not chosen!) a dull one.

· ❧ ·

An imitation of clarity may be the best act we ever did, but it's still an act.

Stepping in the Mud

You can't help someone out of the mud unless you get mud on yourself.
                                          —DAVID BAKSAN

Those who best understand addictions are those who are themselves recovering from their own. This is why the Twelve-Step program has proved so effective. We cannot give someone else something we don't have ourselves.

· ⚘ ·

When I "step" in, I have a chance of getting out.

Oneness

As long as I was able to keep my Higher Power "out there," I was able to blame It (Him, Her) for everything. Now that I realize that my Higher Power and I are one, I've had to reorganize, reorganize, and reorganize my thinking.

—AWS

What a dirty trick! If I am one with my Higher Power, I have to take responsibility for my life. There must be a "kinder, gentler way" to go about this. Isn't there anyone out there who is willing to take the blame for my life?

Where are all the good codependents when we need them?

Self-centeredness

I used to worry about how other people perceived me. Then I realized that most of them were worrying about how I perceived them.

—AWS

We become so self-centered that of course we assume that everyone is focusing upon us and that we are essential. When we are self-centered, we are incapable of seeing that others have a life of their own and their own Higher Power. None of us can ultimately be defined by the other. We all struggle with many of the same issues, and none of us do this alone.

• ❧ •

If I worry about how you perceive me, and you worry about how I perceive you, that makes us equals, doesn't it?

Control

I've always looked at death as a failure or something—no control issues here.
—Susan

If we were really living right, we wouldn't have to die. When I view death as a failure, it gets me off the hook of looking at life. If I just do everything right, nothing will go wrong.

· ✻ ·

Sometimes I have some questions about the way I think.

Laughter

"Dreams are the excrement of the mind. Feces are the excrement of the body. Laughter is the excrement of the soul. Unfortunately our system is set up for constipating everyone in it."

—ANNETTE GOODHEART

Addiction destroys our dreaming, it desecrates our body and it devastates our soul. Recovery is multilevel and multidimensional. As we recover, our mind clears and our body heals. Perhaps we need to look to laughter to clear out the excrement of the soul.

· 🌿 ·

It's time for an enema of the soul.

December

·🌿·

Starting Recovery

TWELVE-STEP BEGINNER: *How long does recovery take?*

OLD-TIMER: *About as long as you are.*
—ANONYMOUS

Recovery is one of the many things we have to start in life before we are there. Of course when we get there, we realize we're just starting.

· ✢ ·

Recovering is a process. Living is a process. We never really "get there" with either one.

Being Ourselves

I'm not really eccentric. I'm just a little different.

—AWS

Being ourselves, we often run the risk of being different. What a hoot! As if any of us weren't different!

Why is it we spend so much time and effort trying to be like others when we have the rare opportunity just to be ourselves? Seems strange, doesn't it?

· ·

I may be a little weird, but then the Creator obviously has quite an imagination.

Bullshitting

I had a man for a sponsor who had bullshit filters in his ears, so he could translate what I said.
—SAM MEIER (SERENITY SAM)

There's a high tolerance for bullshitting in this society. That's one of the reasons we can stay in our disease as long as we can.

· 🌿 ·

Sponsors with bullshit filters are gifts from God. Show your appreciation!

Thinking Addiction

Even with your head in the sand, you can't miss a kick in the ass.

—AWS

Yes, but when I get a kick in the ass, I want to know who gave the kick, what the hidden meaning was behind it, if it was really meant for me, and how I should react. I need to *think* about it.

• ❧ •

Whew! I can see why it's "progress, not perfection" that's important.

Marriage

We have a few short rounds now and again, we have a few long rounds now and again—that's called communicating. Our marriage is built on imperfection. She goes to four or five Alanon meetings a week, and I go to four or five Alcoholics Anonymous meetings a week. We don't have time for all that nitpicking.
—DAVID ORONOFSKY

When we let go of what marriage *should* be and let marriage be what it *is,* we have a chance for marriage to be what it *can* be.

· ✣ ·

Two masks cannot a marriage make. I have to be present with myself to be there for another.

The "Right" Way to Do It

There's another gripe I have: All this talk about dysfunctional families seems to suggest that there are functional *families somewhere. Tell me, how many have* you *seen lately?*

—AWS

We so long for a "right" way, a model, someone to show us how to do it, and we'll *do* it. Why is it so hard just to live our lives?

· 🌿 ·

Longing for the right answer has kept me from discovering the answers that are already there.

Humor

A sense of humor . . . is the ability to understand a joke . . . and that joke is oneself.
—CLIFTON FADIMAN

We know that we are recovering when we gradually develop the ability to see how funny we are when we are in our disease.

· ❧ ·

This disease is *serious,* but *we* don't always have to be.

Illusions

I understand that the majority of the romantic poetry is odes to dead virgins. Now, that's the darnedest thing. What would anyone do with a dead virgin?

—AWS

Aren't illusions grand? They keep us from having to deal with anything but the illusion. Of course, illusions are hard to eat, difficult to sleep with, and they definitely don't relate well. Who ever met an illusion that would tell us the truth or be there when the going gets rough?

· 🌿 ·

Dead virgins are fine in their place, but that place is probably under glass next to the stuffed pheasant.

Living Life

Life is a sexually transmitted disease.
—GUY BELLAMY

If life is a sexually transmitted disease, maybe that explains why there is so much resistance to it in this society. On the other hand, being sexually transmitted and all should engender a certain interest in it. Of course I can start it without wanting to *do* it.

· ☘ ·

Sometimes I catch some things I don't want to, and life is one of them.

Competition

People don't leave our family system, they die out of it. I am so afraid my dad will beat me to it.

—Susan

S ometimes we work so hard on the wrong things. When we compete for the bottom rung, we never climb the ladder.

· ❦ ·

In competition there are no winners.

Vulnerability

I know a man who could make an armored car look vulnerable.
—ANONYMOUS

When we feel so vulnerable, it's hard to *be* vulnerable. As we *are* less vulnerable, we can *be* more vulnerable. Nobody ever said living was logical.

· ❧ ·

Recovery is expanded, open vulnerability.

Laughing at Ourselves

The other day I saw the most hilarious addict:
I looked in the mirror.
—AWS

We really are funny. The more serious we get about our disease, the funnier we get. Have you ever watched an addict switch into "control mode"? We believe that we can control everything and we'll die trying. Now, that's funny!

· ⚘ ·

When I begin to see how funny addictions are, I can be sure I am recovering. Next comes seeing how funny *I* am.

Life

Life is not a suicide mission, nor a dress rehearsal.
—JOYCE

It seems that we are always clearer on what life isn't than on what it is. By the time we complete our list of what life isn't, it will be over. Well, that rules out two favorite possibilities. How many more are there? Perhaps it would be more useful to experience what it *is* than to list what it isn't.

· ❧ ·

When I am really busy living my life, I don't have time to worry about what it isn't.

Comparison

*Part of my ego is into being better and
smarter than others and—it ain't easy.*

—ANONYMOUS

Comparison is part of the disease. When I am
looking "out there," I'm not being "in
here," and if I'm not in here, there's no one to
look out there.

• 🌿 •

Recovery is getting our "in here's" and our
"out there's" straight.

Progress

Whenever things get good for me, I tend to shoot myself in the foot. I'm not ready to get rid of the gun, but at least I can load it with blanks.

—ANONYMOUS

Progress, not perfection, is what we strive for. When I think I have to do all my recovery at once, I forget that it took me years to develop the expertise I have with this disease.

· 🌿 ·

It may not be much, baby, but the movement I am making is all the movement I can muster today. Just for today, I'm sure it's enough.

Recovery

True irreverence is disrespect for another man's God.

—MARK TWAIN

When we disrespect another's God, we have lost touch with our own. When we lose touch with our own God, we have lost touch with ourselves.

· ❧ ·

We have much to recover and we have much to recover from.

Abandoning Ourselves

I am a wonderful place to visit, but I don't want to live here very long. —ANONYMOUS

Sometimes it feels like the kindest thing we can do for ourselves is to "move out," and of course that's exactly what addicts do. We worry about abandonment because we are always abandoning ourselves.

· ❧ ·

I am the only one who can abandon myself.

Confusion

If there's one thing a drinking drunk ain't gonna do, he ain't gonna ask where he is when he doesn't know *where he is.*
—DAVID ORONOFSKY

How often we have had to wait, psych out the situation, look for clues. We have become experts at not knowing where we are when we are there.

· 🌱 ·

Covering up our confusion leads to confusion.

Killing Ourselves

Did you ever notice that burnout and body odor have the same initials? How much time would you want to spend with a person who has either?
—HAL SCHIPPITS

We have many ways of killing ourselves, some quicker than others. Addicts are quite inventive at developing new forms of suicide.

· ༀ ·

Pressure-cooker people are pitiful purveyors of peaceful pastimes.

Amends

PERSON 1: *I have half an amend to make.*

PERSON 2: *I accept it with half of yes.*
—KATIE AND BARB

If we make half-assed amends we'll half-way recover. But half measures availeth nothing.

• ❧ •

An amend to you is an amend to myself. Haven't we shortchanged ourselves enough?

Leaning on Others

If you are not leaning, no one will ever let you down.
—Robert Anthony

How difficult it is to learn how to have others in our life and not smother them with dependency or give ourselves away in dependency! Taking responsibility (ownership) for our lives is not always easy.

· 🌱 ·

The Tower of Pisa is the only thing I know that can lean and still stand on its own.

Rightness

A fanatic is one who can't change his mind and won't change the subject.
—WINSTON CHURCHILL

I t's not that we believe that others are always wrong, we just feel that for whatever reason, we have a greater probability of being right.

· ✣ ·

The righter we are with ourselves, the less we have to *be* right.

Anger

Beware of the furor of a patient man.
—JOHN DRYDEN

Beware of the furor of a patient woman. Rage is no respecter of sex, color, class, or position.

· ❧ ·

Niceness is *not* next to godliness. It's often next to a volcano.

Leap of Faith

We need leaps of faith to take the Steps.

—AWS

Working the Steps is not always easy, and leaping the Steps is impossible!

• ❧ •

The only useful leap in recovery is a leap of faith.

Gifts

My bottom was the gift of desperation.
—DEAN C., AS QUOTED IN *Recovering*

If we were not so stubborn and controlling and so steeped in our denial, our "gifts" would probably not have to hit us with so much force. Yet the force of our desperation is custom-made.

• 🌿 •

Gifts come in many forms. This holiday season, living in the present is the best present of all.

Being Stupid

The difference between genius and stupidity is that genius has its limits.
—Anonymous

Part of our stupidity has been to test to see if our stupidity has limits. We became so arrogant in our disease that we had lost the ability to be realistic about ourselves.

· 🌿 ·

Recovery gives us the genius of knowing our limits, and limits aren't so bad.

Letting Go

Early in recovery I could see the value in the Twelve-Step program, but I thought it just needed a little shaping by me. It certainly has improved since I have been working it.

—AWS

It is amazing how the things that desperately needed our "gentle touch" have improved over the years. When we got busy with our recovery, they just seemed to improve on their own.

· 🌿 ·

When I do my own work, there is less that needs my attention.

Rightness

I don't trust my intuition because I want to be right.
—Betty W.

"Good thinking!" frequently gets us in trouble. What a mess! We don't trust our intuition because we want to be right and our intuition is probably the "rightest" information we have.

· 🌿 ·

The problem is . . . this kind of "good thinking" sounds perfectly logical to an addict.

When logic gets in the way of my intuition, I'm in trouble.

Control

I came to this workshop to learn how to control my controlling.

—BARBARA

Aren't we a hoot! Our illusion of control dies hard. We get a modicum of sobriety and we get cocky. We finally get the idea that we are controllers and we believe that we can control our controlling. It takes us a while to realize that we are also powerless over our controlling . . . too.

· 🌿 ·

When I try to control my need to control, I better get to a meeting.

Living For And Through Others

What is the definition of a co-dependent (relationship addict)? Someone who, when they are dying, has someone else's life flash before their eyes.

—ANONYMOUS

In our disease, we have long since become divorced from our life and have accepted the option of living someone else's. This, of course, takes us off the hook of showing up for our own.

Maybe there's a way we can work this out satisfactorily . . . Let's see . . . if I live yours . . . and you live hers . . . and she lives his and they live ours and we live theirs . . . maybe we could all live happily in an addictive society.

· 🌿 ·

Here's an original thought—What would happen if we each just lived our own life?

Shame

*I used to spend New Year's Day downtown
with all those other sheepish-looking people,
looking for where we parked the car.*

— ROBERT ORBEN

It's nice to have company . . . and there are lots
around willing to share our disease. Unfortunately we never connect. Ending the old year and
beginning the new can be a time for sharing and
connecting. *Happy New Year* doesn't have to be
synonomous with *unconscious*. Facing the terror
of intimacy could be the start of a New Year.

· 🌿 ·

When I don't know where I am, I don't
know who I'm with.

Index